HOW TO DIVORCE WELL

A GUIDE TO SURVIVING & THRIVING ON THE OTHER SIDE

STACEY WALLER

First published by Ultimate World Publishing 2024
Copyright © 2024 Stacey Waller

ISBN

Paperback: 978-1-922597-45-8
Ebook: 978-1-922597-46-5

Stacey Waller has asserted her rights under the Copyright, Designs and Patents Act 1988 to be identified as the author of this work. The information in this book is based on the author's experiences and opinions. The publisher specifically disclaims responsibility for any adverse consequences which may result from use of the information contained herein. Permission to use information has been sought by the author. Any breaches will be rectified in further editions of the book.

All rights reserved. No part of this publication may be reproduced, stored in or introduced into a retrieval system, or transmitted in any form, or by any means (electronic, mechanical, photocopying, recording or otherwise) without the prior written permission of the author. Any person who does any unauthorized act in relation to this publication may be liable to criminal prosecution and civil claims for damages. Enquiries should be made through the publisher.

Cover design: Charlene Rasco
Layout and typesetting: Ultimate World Publishing
Editor: Vanessa McKay

WHAT OTHERS ARE SAYING...

"Why is there nothing on the market like this book? It has tangible tools to walk through each step of a divorce, and it guides us into our next season of life. It's almost like Stacey is holding your hand. She doesn't allow the reader to race through the process or bypass the healing. It's the right blend of tools you can use while illuminating the road ahead to give us goals to strive toward. She's a testimony to this working in her own life. I am inspired and hopeful."

— **Julie Jenkins**

"Stacey's program gave me guidance through my divorce that I didn't realize I needed. With her help, I was able to identify the stage I was in and prepare for what would likely come next. Stacey's sincere concern for my wellbeing was a blessing during a tough time."

— **Alex Robinson**

"This is so TOTALLY amazing Stacey. What struck me when I read this is how much you hurt when you go through a divorce and how "living and active" the word of God is - how that Word got me through some of my hardest seasons. Because I didn't feel as welcome in the church during that season, I spent a lot of time in bars with friends where I kept saying I felt less judgment. Having a book on divorcing well from a believer is SO needed. I desperately needed a bridge for me between my faith and my Christian community and my divorce. I'm so excited for this book and how God will use it for encouragement and emotional and spiritual healing."

— **Karen Jepsen**

"This book is personal experience at its best! It's real and authentic just like the author. Stacey jumps into the hole with each and every reader to give them the confidence to gain their own personal power as she has done through her own journey. She keeps you engaged and looking forward to the next step. It's relatable and heartfelt with the utmost integrity of someone who has been in and out of the deep hole of divorce."

— **Gail Garceau**

"This is so good. Stacey really understood where I was, and she knew what I was feeling. I felt alone. Using the book while working with Stacey helped me uncover and change patterns I hadn't realized were keeping me from moving on. My situation is not completely resolved, but I am becoming more confident and courageous through it - my daughter even sees it. This book is going to help so many people."

- **Nissa Robinson**
How to Divorce Well 1-on-1 Coaching Client

"Oh, how I wish this book had been in print 25 years ago when I went through my own divorce. This wise and heartfelt guide is a long time coming. We can hope and pray that divorce doesn't happen, but when it does, people need the support, wisdom, and tools to know what to do. In a way that feels like you're working with both a loving friend and a wise advocate, Stacey uses a step-by-step, scripture-based, and very practical approach to help us navigate what can be the most traumatic time of life many of us will ever face. This book helps renew our hope and reminds us that as challenging as it might be to navigate, "there is 'a new life worth living' after divorce."

- **Dr. Cheri O'Nan,**
Leadership Development Consultant, Franklin Covey

CONTENTS

What others are saying...	iii
Foreword	1
Dedication	5
Preface	7
Introduction	9
Chapter 1: What Just Happened!?! Where am I?	11
Chapter 2: What Do I Do First?	21
Chapter 3: Why Can't I Move On?	41
Chapter 4: Who Can I Trust?	73
Chapter 5; This HURTS! Cut it out!	95
Chapter 6: Pause! STOP HERE.	121
Chapter 7: I Don't Like the Me I See	133
Chapter 8: Get Me Outta Here!	147
Chapter 9: What Do I Tell People?	161
Chapter 10: Ooooh! How Exciting!	175
Chapter 11: Getting' What I Want! (Laser Focus on 2.0 version of YOU)	191
Chapter 12: "Celebrate Good Times, COME ON!"	211
Epilogue * "Is that you?"	229
About the Author	233
Acknowledgements	235
References	241

FOREWORD

There are many books I have recommended over the years as a pastor and then there are those books which are must-reads and that is especially true when someone is going through a divorce. The reason I mentioned this, is the fact that I just put down the manuscript of Stacey Waller's book **How to Divorce Well: A Guide to Surviving and Thriving on the Other Side**. Stacey was one of those people who I met years ago and as I listened to her story, I realized she had a great deal to say to those navigating the challenges and pitfalls of divorce. She watched her parents go through a divorce and do it in such a way that it didn't damage the kids because they chose not to undercut each other and do what was in the best interest of the kids. That experience as a child coupled with the fact that she would be challenged by her own divorce and follow the same example of her parents as she went through the divorce uniquely qualified Stacey to write this book.

Not only was I fascinated by her story and the healing God brought to her over the years. As I have listened to her story and observed her life, it's no wonder she wrote this incredibly insightful and practical book. She is the real deal, with a real story, and real godly wisdom.

When she asked me to write this forward I did so with a great deal of humility, because she thought me worthy of such a privilege, but also bold confidence because I know the truths in this book have the potential to radically change your life. Like Stacey, I watched my parents navigate their divorce, but unlike her, my parents didn't do it well, and we kids suffered. Even though I became a Christian at the age of 17, there was much internal work that needed to be done. I was broken and blind and that affected every significant relationship in my life. Looking back, I wish my parents had a level of practical wisdom and guidance as they went through their divorce which would have prevented the pain we kids experienced.

This is where Stacey's book **How to Divorce Well** comes in. It is chapter after chapter of wisdom that will help you pinpoint practical steps you can take to heal through your journey of divorce, to open your eyes to how you can resist the temptation to throw your spouse under the bus, especially with the kids. When it comes to divorce, as hard as it might be, kids are the orphans and parents have the opportunity to protect them and minimize the impact from the divorce.

Stacey has done her part in providing the wisdom as she guides you through your divorce, but you have to do your part in reading and then applying the principles and truths to your daily life experience. You have to implement the concepts, tools, and activities week by week. Having watched other divorces navigate a healthy divorce when it comes to their kids, I can assure you the principles and wisdom from this book work.

FOREWORD

I love the fact that Stacey has drawn from both her parents' example and her own to give you a challenge to do the same. Jesus proclaimed "The truth will set you free." Do you want to be free of negative self-talk, do you want to be free from the lies you have believed about yourself and your spouse, do you want to be free to have healthy and vibrant relationships with others after your divorce, do you want to protect the very souls of your children, then Stacey's book is a must-read. No one wants to go through a divorce, but if you find yourself in that position, at least consider **How to Divorce Well**.

I am proud to know Stacey well, and excited to highly recommend her book. I know the wisdom and direction she provides are time-tested, she is proof of the axiom that you can lead from where you have been!

Sincerely

Eric C. Heard
Pastor of Stewardship and Pastoral Ministry
Mariners Church
Irvine, California

DEDICATION

I dedicate this book to my mom and dad. My parents divorced when I was young, yet I felt I had the world's greatest childhood. They got along, always spoke respectfully of each other, and wouldn't let me disrespect the other. As a child, I honestly had no idea that coming from a divorced family wasn't ideal.

Little did I know my parents were both still hurt, often didn't respect what the other was doing, and they apparently disagreed all the time. I had no clue because they agreed in the divorce to do two things:

- Always provide a united front to me.
- Speak respectfully of one another.

I guess it worked because my childhood memories of them are wonderful ones, and I was very close with each of them. They divorced so well it inspired this book.

Mom and Dad, I am honored and so grateful to be your daughter. This book is dedicated to you.

HOW TO DIVORCE WELL

This book is also dedicated to YOU. You're either beginning a journey, in the middle of it, or looking back on it, and you're wanting to do it well. This book is filled with not only my and my parent's stories but also includes the contributions of many men and women who were willing to share what they did well, and what they wish they would've done differently.

May you learn from our regrets and gain courage from our successes.

Mom, Dad and myself circa 1972

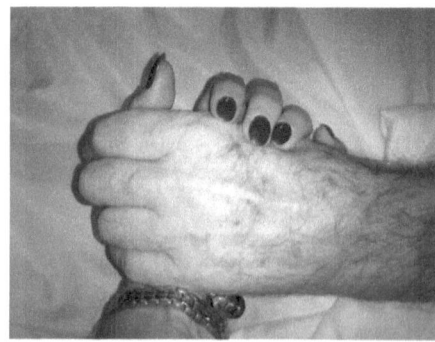

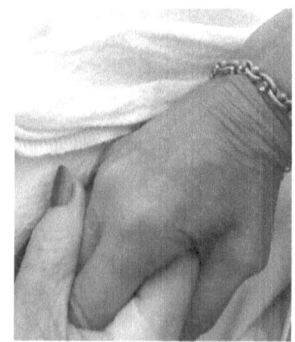

Dad   Mom

PREFACE

People always say, "Everyone has a book in them." I sure understand that because I have for over 30 years. My parents divorced when I was a young child. If you asked me before my mid-20s, I could've convinced you that having divorced parents was THE BEST! I thought people were secretly envious of me because it was so great to have divorced parents. You get individual time with each of them, they get along well, and you have twice the fun!

Little did I know, divorce was not ideal. My parents did it so well they had me fooled. When they told me their sides of the story in my 20s, I asked them how they did it and what their secret strategy was. They let me know they often disagreed, they just didn't let me hear or see it. They agreed to present a united front and to disagree behind the scenes. They also agreed to not speak poorly of each other in front of me. Indeed, that provided a healthy, strong foundation for a crumbled, broken home. I always said I wanted to write the book, "How to Divorce Well," based on their example.

Fast-forward 30 years and my own marriage of 20 years suddenly ended. I found myself looking back at what my parents had done, but in complete disbelief at how hard it was to be nice, to agree behind the scenes, and to show a united front to the kids. My parents became more heroic in my eyes as I felt like a complete failure: incompetent, scared, and vulnerable. I quickly realized it's much easier to watch someone else do something hard than to do it myself.

I knew it could be done. However, I knew if I started making decisions the way I felt in that moment, I was not going to do it well. I knew I would not give my kids the best chance of having the kind of childhood I enjoyed. I also knew I wouldn't be able to be proud of myself for taking the high road, like my parents had done.

So, I started doing what I remembered my parents doing, and resisting what was easiest (getting angry, venting to people to share my side, or simply running away). Don't get me wrong; many days I did do all those things – cuss and scream my brains out and worse – but I wrote notes as I did. These were honest notes of what worked, and what didn't. As psychologist and TV show host, Dr. Phil McGraw says, "So, how's that workin' for ya?" I've also asked other divorced friends what worked and what hasn't worked for them. Our stories are shared on the pages ahead.

Maybe someone bought this book for you, or maybe you're going through it with a group at church or another support organization. My desire for you is that you learn from our mistakes and consider what we've done well. My prayer is for you to start ten steps ahead of us. The following pages are filled with the ten keys to surviving divorce and building a new life worth living... and YOU CAN DO IT. I'm with you all the way. Let's do this!

INTRODUCTION

This guy is walking down the street when he falls into a hole. The walls are so steep, he can't get out. A doctor passes by. Our guy yells up, 'Hey doc, can you help me out?' The doctor writes a prescription, throws it down in the hole and moves on.

Then a priest comes along and the guy shouts out, 'Father, I'm down in this hole. Can you help me out?' The priest writes out a prayer, throws it down in the hole and moves on.

Then a friend walks by, 'Ed, it's me, can you help me out?' And the friend jumps in the hole. Our guy says, 'Are you STUPID? Now we're both down here!' The friend says, 'Yeah, but I've been down here before, and I know the way out.

Thanks for opening this book. Thank you for allowing me to jump into the hole with you. Now, you're not alone. I've been down here before, and I know the way out.

HOW TO DIVORCE WELL

First, a bit about me.
I am not:
- a licensed therapist,
- an attorney,
- a theologian.

I am:
- divorced, even though I didn't want to be,
- a child of a healthy divorce,
- experiencing a healthy divorce.

To be clear, I'm not licensed to give psychological advice, just share my and others' experiences. I'm also not licensed to give legal advice, just share my and others' cases. I also don't offer a theological justification for or against divorce.

My heart's desire is for you to find the health and healing I and others have found during and after a divorce. I want to offer you a peek into our inner lives – our feelings, our good and bad choices, and both our triumphs and tribulations in the process of our divorces. My prayer is for one person (hopefully you) to do something that makes your landing softer and easier than many of the stories you will read in the pages to follow.

Now, let's get out of this hole together!

WALLER

CHAPTER 1

WHAT JUST HAPPENED!?! WHERE AM I?

"Almost everything will work again if you unplug it for a few minutes, including you."
— **Anne Lamott**

"I wake up at 3am in complete shock and fear. Most nights I'm not even able to get to sleep."

"So many things are out of my control. With so many changes, I feel completely unstable and insecure."

"I just want to get this over with and be able to start a new relationship. I'm fine!"

Sound familiar? When going through a divorce, many of us experience the same fears, racing thoughts, and feelings. We often bounce between fear and future tripping, getting caught up in worst-case scenarios. Others just want to fill that void and avoid the feeling of emptiness altogether. The loneliness can feel debilitating and can easily lead us to look for someone or something else to fill that gaping hole.

Let's see if you can relate. These are the five stages I found I went through during my divorce. At any given time, I was in the middle of one of these stages or had one foot in one stage and one foot in the next stage.

STAGES OF GOING THROUGH A DIVORCE:
- Stage 1: Wake-up/Shock
- Stage 2: Triage/Prioritize
- Stage 3: Breathe/Stabilize
- Stage 4: Make yourself marketable in your business and personal life
- Stage 5: Step out as the new, independent 2.0 version of yourself

Which stage do you feel you're in? Are you between two? Take the free assessment at www.HowToDivorceWell.com

In my divorce journey, I was very impatient at first. I was so frustrated that moving through the stages took time. I don't know if it was pride or insecurity, but probably a combination of both. I sure didn't like when a close friend told me, "It's

WHAT JUST HAPPENED!?! WHERE AM I?

going to take you at least a year to get over this." WHAT!?! No. I didn't have a year! I needed the new 2.0 version of me and the 2.0 version of my life to start NOW! I couldn't afford to wait years to get through this. But it turned out that he was right – except he was gracious enough to say one year, when it was closer to two or three.

Going through each stage is a process, and it is true that for everything, there is a season:

> "…A right time to cry and another to laugh,
> A right time to lament and another to cheer."
> (Ecclesiastes 3:4-5 MSG)

You might just be starting the process of divorce. Maybe you've known you were going to do this for months or years, so you have a plan and can zip through stages one and two. You don't need to **wake up** or recognize you're in **shock**. You have probably already **triaged and prioritized** what needed to be done first. You may have had a chance to **breathe**. Maybe now you're already stabilizing and regaining your self-esteem to **market** yourself as an independent person. You're ready to step out and be the new, **2.0 version of yourself.**

Let's begin, however, by understanding the first two stages.

STAGE 1: WAKE-UP/SHOCK

Feeling lost, confused, and shattered? Sometimes the greatest leap of faith you make in this stage will be getting out of bed.

If you're in this stage, you probably haven't bought this book for yourself. A friend likely saw the book as an aid for a path to relief, and you ended up with a copy. When I was in this stage, having "clarity of mind" wouldn't have described me well. If you're in the Wake-Up/Shock stage, I'm SO grateful you're reading this. YOU are my WHY. It took courage for you to open these pages. I am proud of you and happy for you. Just remember you're going to get through this, you're going to be okay, you're going to thrive again. Now, keep reading.

The Wake-Up/Shock stage is normally the response we have when we are not the ones initiating the divorce or separation. When it initially happened, it felt like a gut punch and I was in shock. I had to actually wake up and recognize it was happening. I had to look at the reality.

Then again, you may have initiated the separation. No matter how you've found yourself here, including couples who were equally seeking the divorce, each person I've spoken with has described at some point thinking:

"This can't be happening!"

However, you've found yourself here, you're left in shock and you're in the process of waking up and getting your bearings. It's time to come to terms with a new reality and ACT as if there's nothing you can do to make them come

WHAT JUST HAPPENED!?! WHERE AM I?

back or remind yourself of the reasons you had to separate. If this sounds like your current situation, you're standing in the Wake-Up/Shock stage.

"Where do I start? "

"I have so many things I'm stressed out about. I can't seem to get anything done."

"My To-Do List gets longer and longer. It seems every time I get a few things done, 10 more are added."

"The amount of what I need to do is just overwhelming, and I don't know where to start. Most days, I just put the covers back over my head and stay in bed all day."

I get it. I was there. This is when we need to focus on doing the most important things first, right? But what's most important?

STAGE 2: TRIAGE/PRIORITIZE

The key to this stage is to use the few moments of clarity you have to write down your priorities. For example:

- I stay alive.
- I have a roof over my head.
- I have a way to support myself.

Those were my priorities, except I have kids, so they were included in the above.

The definition of the word triage by Merriam-Webster is: "The sorting and allocation of treatment to patients and especially battle and disaster victims according to a system of priorities designed to maximize the number of survivors."

I don't know how you're feeling, but I felt like a disaster victim after a battle during this stage.

First, just continue to remind yourself you're already a survivor. Next, we need to maximize the allocation of your energy to the priorities which will ensure a solid foundation for your successful next chapter.

For me, the three priorities above were the beginning of my triage stage. I stay alive, I have a roof over my head, and I have a way to support myself. I spent quite a long time here. I had one foot in wake-up/shock and one foot in triage. Let's unpack what questions I needed to answer:

- ☐ I stay alive.
  - What am I doing that keeps me alive mentally and emotionally?
  - Worrying about the future (other stages) is what wakes me up in the middle of the night. Do I have a good way to get back to sleep? What gives me rest?
  - What feeds my physical needs for sustenance?

If you answer these questions with unhealthy coping mechanisms, it's common. This is YOUR journey. You will

WHAT JUST HAPPENED!?! WHERE AM I?

have YOUR story, and you know what it takes for YOU to get through this. Obviously, the hope is that unhealthy coping mechanisms will not remain part of your full story, as coping mechanisms can stunt our movement through the stages. However, whatever it takes to keep you alive is okay for now.

We do have tools we can use to get us out of being stuck in the triage stage. We have a route free of damaging coping mechanisms. There is a path to version 2.0 of yourself and your new life. However, the key to this stage is staying on this earth and breathing. Whatever it takes for you to stay alive and breathing, you need to do it.

Put a checkmark if you feel confident that this has been/is being accomplished:

- ☐ I have a roof over my head
  - The mortgage/rent is going to be paid.
  - I can rely on my soon-to-be-ex to pay their part.
  - I have other options (Plan B) I can consider.
  - I feel safe in my home (physical security).
- ☐ I have a source of income
  - I have a source of creating my own income (this may include unemployment).
  - I have my own bank account, possibly at a separate bank or credit union.
  - I have my own individual budget.
- ☐ My basic needs are met (food/utilities/gas/transportation)
  - There is enough food in the home.
  - I am able to pay my utilities.
  - I am able to afford gas in my car or easily use another form of transportation.

HOW TO DIVORCE WELL

If people in your life are offering help, it's a good time to consider accepting it. For me, the answer during this stage was, "Yes. Please. Thank you." Although we don't want to feel like we are becoming a burden to others during this initial stage, it is a comfort and often necessary to ask for and receive help.

"Okay, I'm alive, but I sure don't feel like it. I need to know how to live... alone."

Well, first of all, CONGRATULATIONS! It takes strength to just be a survivor. Take a minute and pat yourself on the back.

What you've done by making sure the most important things are done is incredible, and many people don't get this far, or they focus on the urgent and unimportant "To Dos" and get distracted from the important. I'm proud of you, and most importantly, I hope *you're* proud of you!

WHAT JUST HAPPENED!?! WHERE AM I?

LET'S PUT IT TO WORK:

I have determined which stage I'm in, or the two I'm currently between (identify now).

- I triaged and I'm focusing my time, attention and energy on my (and my children's) physical needs.
- I have a specific plan of action and a list of people to contact to address the gaps I've identified and prioritized.

Now, time to start feeling like we're alive again! That's what Stage 3 – Breathe/Stabilize is for.

In the next chapter, we learn to start living again. See you there!

Take the questionnaire here

CHAPTER 2

WHAT DO I DO FIRST?

Were you like me and experience any of this?

> "I might be surviving, but I have a constant pit in my stomach."

> "My stress is through the roof! With all the 'what ifs' running through my head, I'm foggy brained and not functioning."

> "I'm alive, but I don't know why. I don't want to get out of bed. Some days I don't."

Yeah, I was there too. But keep reading. It will get better, I promise. In Stage 3, we discover how to start living and functioning again. We need to start somewhere, and Triage

HOW TO DIVORCE WELL

and Prioritize is where we start – YOUR safety (and your kids if you're a parent) is number one. We are going to stay awake and alive through this divorce! We are not going to let it take us down!

GOOD JOB!

After we've focused intensely on our survival priorities, let's plan how to effectively operate in our third stage.

STAGE 3: BREATHE/STABILIZE

Okay, I've woken up from the shock. I'm working on the triage.

BREATHE: To relax after being frightened or tense about something... but how?

What do I do to breathe? What does it look like to do this right?

> **HINT**
> This stage, and what we learn here, continues to help us throughout all five stages.

WHAT DO I DO FIRST?

SEVEN FAST-TRACK FIXES TO BE ABLE TO BREATHE AGAIN

1. Breathe: Pen to Paper

The quickest way to calm my racing thoughts and fears was by writing. Yep, putting pen to paper. Sometimes I wrote in a stream of consciousness or vented anger. Other times I made a list of everything that made me mad – it helped me feel justified in my anger.

If I had a looming decision, sometimes I wrote a list of pros and cons. Whatever was spinning in my mind, I found it incredibly therapeutic to write it out. The amount of time it took to go from my head through my hands and onto paper was enough time to eventually get clarity. Other times, after waking up in the middle of the night, it was just enough to vent on paper so I could get back to sleep. Sometimes writing resulted in formulating new ideas or unique perspectives on old problems.

Although many of us have an aversion to journaling as it reminds us of the childish "Dear Diary," we can also think of it as getting it out of our head and keeping a logbook of our thoughts. Truth is there are healing effects of physically writing our thoughts and feelings.

My journaling was usually in the form of "Dear God…"
My journaling was honest.
My journaling was raw.
My journaling included questions.
My journaling wasn't free of expletives.

HOW TO DIVORCE WELL

That's just me, maybe that's not comfortable for you. I found the more honest and raw I was with my thoughts, the more I was able to acknowledge the depth of pain, process the feelings, accept my reality, and seek solutions as I moved through the gut-wrenching process of divorce.

Some people like to type, but when we write pen to paper there is no opportunity to delete – only cross out. Keeping those journals can be helpful to look back and see our train of thought (and progress) as time passes.

Now it's your turn:

Grab a journal, or plan to set aside some time tonight and write out things like:

- What's making me angry right now?
- What am I fearful of in this situation?
- What doesn't make sense about what's happening, or why it's happening to me?

After you've journaled, come back to this list and see if you can circle a few of these adjectives that describe what you've written:

Realistic, bare, brutal, frank, unembellished, gritty, blunt, direct, harsh, genuine, sincere, uninhibited, transparent, blatant, unfiltered, point-blank, plain-speaking, not beating about the bush, pure, authentic, unmodified, brutally honest, and telling it like it is.

Does your journal entry pass the test?

Great, continue...

If not, just keep in mind this is your goal. Why? Because we cannot fix what we do not acknowledge.

2. Breathe: Affirmations

For me, the key in this stage was to develop daily affirmations. A close friend FORCED me to come up with three statements about myself that were positive, and I had to say them to myself every morning when I woke up before my feet hit the ground.

Write them if you're struggling to say them, but work up the courage to say them out loud. What are daily affirmations? Think of the 80s skit on Saturday Night Live: "I'm good enough, I'm smart enough, and doggone it, people like me!" That's pretty close to what they sound like and we'll work on them more specifically in an upcoming chapter, but for now, let's come up with three daily affirmations. If you're like me and need someone else to tell you what to say, you can borrow a few that were my starters:

- I am enough.
- I am a strong independent woman.
- I am a committed and connected mom.

Now it's your turn:

1. _____

2. _____

3. _____

p.s. Say them, even when you don't believe them yet. I did. Now I believe them.

3. Breathe: Self Care and Sleep

My mom used to tell me that sometimes I needed to think of myself as a sponge. She said if you give and give and give, you become empty and drained, like a dried-out sponge. Just like a sponge, it needs to take in water to be useful.

When we're in the emotionally draining situation of a divorce, we're drained – wiped out. She also used to say, "You need to learn when to stop and learn to soak in. You can't keep going forever." That was her way of saying it's important to know when it's time to take care of yourself.

What if you feel that you don't have time for self-care? If you don't, all else will be slower and harder. You're more productive after you practice self-care. What if you can't afford it? You can't afford not to. Self-care doesn't have to be expensive. You can afford something small, like a bubble bath. It doesn't cost much! Some simple ideas might include:

- Take deep breaths. Hold your breath and exhale.
- Watch something that makes you laugh.
- Light a candle.
- Put on some fun music and dance.
- Take a 30-minute walk or jog in nature.
- Write down three things you're grateful for today.
- Cook and sit down to eat your favorite nutritious meal.
- Travel to visit a friend.
- Buy yourself something new you use often (wallet, walking shoes, keychain, etc.).

WHAT DO I DO FIRST?

Write three ideas for self-care that are feasible within your time and financial constraints:

DAILY IDEAS

1. _____

2. _____

3. _____

WEEKLY IDEAS

1. _____

2. _____

3. _____

MONTHLY/YEARLY IDEAS

1. _____

2. _____

3. _____

But I Can't Sleep!

What are your typical solutions when you can't sleep? Turn on the TV? Get up, do something productive to get it off your mind, then have a hard time winding down again? Do you have a sleep app on your phone that helps you wind down? Do you meditate? Take herbal, over the counter, or prescription sleep aids?

I would wake up in fear, worrying about the future. I finally did something that helped. When I'd wake up in the middle of the night paralyzed in fear thinking, "How am I going to pay rent next month?"

I'd write down the fear on a note card. I'd put that card with my fear in my prayer card box by my bed. When I went back to my prayer card box in the morning with my devotions, I changed my fear into a prayer.

For example:

> I'm scared I can't pay rent!

> God, please give me a way to pay rent next month.

It worked.

I found there are all kinds of ways to get back to sleep, but to deny it and just lie awake was counterproductive. Being without sleep made me feel unproductive the following day, which ultimately affected my self-esteem. As there are 24-hour prayer lines available, I even tried calling a prayer line on television for help once. Having someone praying with me in the middle of the night was comforting.

4. Breathe: Counseling

Although friends are great, they are not licensed psychiatrists or psychologists who are not only trained to handle divorce,

WHAT DO I DO FIRST?

but also deal with it frequently and have suggestions for what works and what doesn't.

It's time to focus on you. In a counseling session, we don't ask a counselor, "Well, tell me how your family is doing? Is your mom doing well?" When we're talking with friends, it is a back-and-forth conversation.

> "At the end of the counseling session, we don't ask a counselor, 'Well tell me how your family is doing? Is your mom doing well?'"
>
> #HowToDivorceWell

Counseling is solely focused on YOU. This is self-care.

You may feel that counseling is not feasible for your budget, but there are low to no cost options:

- Check your medical insurance. Many of my clients are surprised to find certain counselors are covered either fully or partially under their policy.
- Local universities have upper-division psychology programs. This is because, as part of their master's programs, students studying to be psychologists do what are called "blind observations." This is when a graduate student is typically your counselor/psychologist while their instructor is on the other side of a darkened window. You receive the counseling you need under the watchful eye of a trained instructor.
- Reach out to a Care Pastor at most any large church, and they will either have in-house counselors, or at least a list of recommended counselors. Some churches even have counseling programs where lay pastors or lay counselors are available at little or no charge.

- If finances are a barrier, you can ask if your favorite therapist works on a "sliding scale." Many counselors have programs to help those who are in a financially challenging season.

Whatever we do, it's critical that we seek help.

5. Breathe: Boundaries

"Boundaries" may sound limiting. Setting good personal boundaries in relationships can prove to be freeing and critical to bolstering our self-esteem. Defining boundaries is determining what behavior you will accept. When we do not develop boundaries, or our boundaries are overstepped, we can easily feel under-appreciated or taken advantage of.

Here are some areas to consider boundaries to determine what you're willing to accept with your former spouse in the future:

- Communication expectations in person, by phone or text.
- Certain topics during discussions (I found it best to stay away from personal issues and kept it very business-like).
- Any kind of intimacy with your spouse during the divorce.
- Requirement for notification/request before entering the previously shared home.
- Use of common bank accounts and credit cards.
- Times and frequency of interaction with your/their family and friends (holidays, etc).
- Times and frequency of interaction with your spouse.

WHAT DO I DO FIRST?

For example:

When our face-to-face conversations became too heated, I changed my boundary to phone conversations only. It was later changed to text only, and when we needed to speak on the phone, we would text ahead with a request to call the other. Phone calls ended up being business-like and were short and became less and less frequent. Other than an emergency, calls and texts were during socially acceptable hours. I made boundaries so I was less likely to be caught off guard, upset, talked into something I'd later regret, or just be unwelcomely bothered.

The overarching concept was, "How can I best maintain my well-being while maintaining open lines of communication and being able to exercise personal self-control?" I quickly learned that certain situations were hot buttons, or triggered me to feel weak, inferior, or scared. Maybe certain situations make you angry quicker:

- Showing up without notice.
- Overstaying their welcome / staying too late.
- Making payments out of the common bank account you hadn't approved.

As those instances arose, I created stronger, more defined boundaries. Some boundaries allowed for a cooling-off period before I needed to respond. For example, changing from phone calls to texts.

> Once I knew the divorce was pending, I was no longer comfortable having sex with my ex.
> #HowToDivorceWell

HOW TO DIVORCE WELL

The boundaries evolved. Some lightened up while others tightened up.

Obviously, my boundaries will differ from yours. The key is to think through these issues before they arise. For instance, once I knew the divorce was pending, I was no longer comfortable having sex with my ex. It would have been too confusing, and opened the opportunity to muddle my emotions thus affecting my ability to think clearly for decision-making. In addition, the longer I kept that door open for an emotional attachment, it would likely just postpone and prolong the inevitable grieving process.

My Boundaries were:
1. No sex or intimacy during divorce.
2. Need notification before coming into the family home.
3. Communication by text only. Phone calls by pre-agreement via text.

Now it's your turn. My boundaries are:

1. _____

2. _____

3. _____

6. Breathe: Legally

Judy's experience broke my heart as her decision had a devastating impact, and it was completely avoidable. She even realized later that she was warned. This is her story:

WHAT DO I DO FIRST?

"When my kids' dad left us unexpectedly, my counselor told me, 'Get a separation immediately. You don't need to divorce quickly, but get a separation right away. In our state, it's not a difficult form to file, and it will give you protection and a chance to breathe.'

I was not even close to being ready to actually consider getting a divorce. I felt like getting a legal separation would just make the idea of divorce more real and more likely. My counselor tried to convince me, saying that as soon as the separation is filed, I would be protected. I was financially strapped and going to do my divorce through one of the online options. Both a divorce and a separation cost the same amount, and I couldn't afford both, so I didn't do the separation.

Well, sure enough, my ex had opened seven credit cards during our separation. In the divorce, I was legally responsible for all those charges, many of which were from him taking women out on the town! Not only was I responsible for half of the debt he had accrued, him opening all those accounts managed to ruin my credit too!

Wow. My counselor was right, and I really regret making choices based on the state of my emotions instead of taking her advice. I'm paying for it now. Literally."

So, because your ex is not with you – either emotionally or physically – they may be acting differently and doing new things that you would never have imagined. When we get a separation, we're not held responsible for those actions and the costs associated with them.

FOLLOW UP TO JUDY'S STORY: Judy later found out that as the credit cards were opened in her ex-husband's name, she was not necessarily responsible for their payment. It was only once these new accounts were included in the divorce, and she had agreed to pay 50% of all debts, she was legally bound to that new debt as well.

What's the Difference Between a Separation and a Divorce?*

There are advantages to obtaining a legal separation while trying to decide whether to divorce. A legal separation can be used as a pausing point on the way to divorce. A legal separation differentiates from a divorce by a matter of degrees.

When legally separated, in many instances you still can benefit from maintaining health insurance and social security benefits, etc. It allows you and your ex time to come to an agreement about issues like childcare and personal budgets. Legally, the marriage remains intact while allowing you and your ex time to decide the next best steps forward. Simultaneously, in many cases, it can protect either of you from many financial obligations which are run up after the separation is filed. A legal separation is reversible. A divorce is not. Legal separations may also be easier for the children, as you stay married, and it does not sound as overwhelming and final as a divorce. Each state has its own laws, and in some areas, after a certain period of time, a legal separation turns into a divorce. Please check with your legal counsel for the specifics in your state.

7. Breathe: Financially

Catherine was leaving her husband because he was both physically and emotionally abusive to her and the kids. She feared for their safety.

> "I knew I was going to leave him. I had to protect my kids. I was doing everything right - so I thought. I had an attorney, I had opened my own checking account, and I had a place set up for the kids and I to move to. One day he unexpectedly came home early and picked up the mail on the way into the house. A letter from my attorney and my new bank statement happened to come that day. All my efforts and all my planning went up in smoke in that moment. He blew up. We had a huge argument, and it was all in front of the kids. I was completely caught off guard. I was defending myself in anger and found myself saying things that would normally not come out of my mouth. I even disclosed things that gave him details of what I knew. I lost my opportunity to have all my ducks in a row in preparation to walk out the door. I was, and still am mortified about some of the things he and I both said. The kids cannot unhear those ugly details."

I wish Catherine would've done one extra step – opened a P.O. Box and pointed all new correspondence to the alternate address. Her husband went on a tirade that was unlike any before. His attorneys quickly got involved and what was a "perfect plan" quickly turned into the perfect storm. He accused her of attempting to kidnap his children and worse.

Top Tips to Protect Yourself Financially

- Contact a financial advisor and discuss a plan.
- Run your plan by your attorney or legal advisor.
- Inventory all assets and obtain appraisals when needed. At minimum, walk around your home with the video function of your phone on and speak about each item.
- Duplicate all important documents (financial, medical, life insurance, travel documents, appraisals, marriage, and birth certificates, etc.)
- If planning on taking time from work, change your emergency contact information to someone other than your ex.
- Open your own checking account.
- Open a P.O. Box.
- Sign up for two free credit monitoring services and check your credit monthly. These services that check your credit do not negatively affect your credit.

In Catherine's unfortunate situation, she was on the right track, but the ensuing divorce became bitter and incredibly expensive. A few key steps could have protected her financially as well.

Karen, a client of my divorcing course, shared her story about her credit:

> "My husband always did the bills. In the middle of our divorce, my car died. I went to our credit union to secure a loan to buy a new car. When they ran my credit, I was mortified – my score was 630! They said I didn't have bad credit; I basically had no credit. Wait

a second: we always paid our bills on time, both our names are on the pink slips for our cars, and both of our names are on the credit union account. Why do I not have a solid credit history? That's when I realized that because all our utilities and car purchases had been solely in my ex-husband's name, I was not building up a credit history.

The loan agent told me she had never seen a one-page credit report in her entire career. They charged me 10.9% interest! Fortunately, because there wasn't a lot on my report, it also made it easier to raise my credit faster, but it still took a couple of years. And when I needed to be saving money the most – at the beginning of the divorce – I was charged the highest interest. One of my biggest regrets in my divorce was not being more involved with my credit during my marriage. It caused me to start out at a place of weakness, and tremendous disadvantage in the divorce."

I find this to be quite common among women in divorce. In fact, not having a solid credit score can be a deterrent to stepping out and becoming confident in our independence.

SECRETS THEIR ATTORNEY DOESN'T WANT YOU TO KNOW:*

In most states, alimony is taxed, child support is not.

For parents, there are often financial benefits to being named head of household in the divorce.

HOW TO DIVORCE WELL

Although child support normally ends when the child is 18, alimony can end based on an agreed upon date or when you remarry.

Please note: I am not authorized nor attempting to give legal or financial advice: this is simply my experience and understanding at the time of writing this book. Please seek professional legal and financial counsel for the best legal and financial advice in your individual situation.

LET'S PUT IT TO WORK:

IF YOU DO NOTHING ELSE, try these three things every day:
1. Say your affirmations before your feet hit the floor.
2. Take a shower every day.
3. Read your list of boundaries every day.

If your day is going awry, think back on these three things.
Did you miss any of them?
That's what the restart button is for.
Take care of you. You're worth it.

- I have determined which stage I'm in, or the two I'm currently between (identify now).

WHAT DO I DO FIRST?

- I triaged and I'm focusing my time, attention and energy on my (and my children's) physical needs.
- I have my boundaries written down.
- I've written down my three daily affirmations.
- I've secured a counselor/therapist if or when I need it.
- I've set up bedside options for middle-of-the-night sleep strategies (an app, paper, and pen).
- I've written down self-care ideas (daily, weekly, and monthly).
- I've taken a shower today!

CHAPTER 3

WHY CAN'T I MOVE ON?

"It's been 10 years and I'm STILL angry!"

"I can't seem to stop obsessing about my ex. What are they doing now? Are they dating someone else? Are they happy and I'm the only one left mad and hurting? I just can't get them out of my mind."

"I'm getting through life just day-to-day, but I just don't have that 'spark' in my life. I feel like my urge to enjoy life has just fizzled."

"How do I get over feeling stuck?"

Do any of these describe how you're feeling right now? Have you overcome all your negative emotions? Or are you where

HOW TO DIVORCE WELL

I was – feeling stuck? Do you seem to find yourself irritable with seemingly unrelated people or situations? Do you find yourself thinking about your ex and secretly hoping they're as miserable as you? Do you find yourself cringing in anger when someone mentions your ex's name?

FRIEND: "Why can't you just forgive them?"
    YOU: "What!?! Don't you know what they did?"
    YOU: "Why? They never asked for forgiveness or even said 'I'm sorry!'"
    YOU: "They don't even recognize what they did was wrong! They don't see the ripple effects."
    YOU: "I can forgive, but I'm not going to forget!"
    YOU: "I don't want to forgive them because it gives them the ability to hurt me again."
    YOU: "How can I forgive if they are not even willing to change?"
    YOU: "I can't forgive. I'm not even sure I'm done hurting yet."
    YOU: "If I forgive, I feel like I'm letting go of the relationship completely. I still want them to come back. Not forgiving is the last thing I hold onto and it's the only way I can keep them in my life."

I learned forgiveness was the solution to getting unstuck, but most of us are nowhere near the point of wanting to do it.

Can you relate to Jim?

> "Each time I would find myself in a circumstance that set me back due to my ex, I'd get mad all over again. In my mind, I'd call her every name in the book, then figure out a way to tell her about my

situation and rub her nose in the fact that she caused all the damage."

What is forgiveness? I like the way Pastor Mike Todd defines forgiveness: "The intentional and voluntary process by which a victim undergoes a change in feelings and attitude regarding an offense and overcomes negative emotions such as resentment and vengeance." The problem is forgiveness isn't easy.

I Don't Want to Forgive!

It's HARD! Why? Forgiveness isn't a one-time action, it's a process. Forgiveness can feel like it makes us vulnerable. Forgiveness requires us to acknowledge a lot of pain. Forgiveness forces us to recognize someone else has the power to hurt us, and that can be hard for our pride to accept.

I found some simple actions to take when I wasn't ready to forgive. The easiest one happened when I realized I didn't need to say anything to my ex. I kept it all in my mind or on paper. I could write it and burn it – which I did!

THREE SIMPLE TIPS TO DO WHEN YOU'RE NOT READY TO FORGIVE

1. Acknowledge that forgiveness and trust are different.

Do you question if you can trust that person in the future? Is that a barrier to forgiving them? That's okay. We can still forgive. For me, this realization was key:

HOW TO DIVORCE WELL

> Forgiveness is for the past.
> Trust is for the future.

> Forgiveness is for the past.
> Trust is for the future.
> #HowToDivorceWell

Forgiveness is for the past.

What has your ex done to you that hurt or angered you? Write a quick list:

1. _____
2. _____
3. _____
4. _____
5. _____
6. _____
7. _____
8. _____
9. _____
10. _____
11. _____
12. _____

A friend helped me see that forgiveness was not me letting them off the hook, but instead letting ME off the hook by allowing me to move forward. It also meant that I didn't need to place my trust in them in the future. With that in mind, I was able to forgive with freedom, but I needed to understand that difference before I could move on.

I love how Dr. Henry Cloud puts it: "Love covers a multitude of sins, but it doesn't overlook a multitude of sins." I've learned that forgiveness was not to say it didn't happen or deny that there are problems. It had nothing to do with the wrongs done to me. I learned that forgiveness needed to happen for *me* – and that means *you* as well. Simply put, we don't want to live in denial, and we also don't want to live in dysfunction. It became abundantly clear that:

- **Forgiveness is not letting them off the hook.**
- **Forgiveness is not trust for the future.**
- **Forgiveness is not a feeling.**
- **Forgiveness can be a continuing process, not just a one-time action.**
- **Forgiveness does not mean reconciliation.** It can, but the terms and concepts are not synonymous. Forgiveness takes one person. Reconciliation takes more than one.

2. Acknowledged past debt can be canceled.

Forgiveness of past pain may be easier to think of as the cancellation of a debt.

HOW TO DIVORCE WELL

Cancelling a debt does not necessarily mean:

- Living as if the debt never happened (rewriting your story).
- Giving another loan (trust for the future).
- Starting a business together (reconciliation).[1]

We can also continue to remind ourselves that our new list of boundaries (which we're reading every day), is providing a fence of protection to help discourage the same offense from happening again. Sometimes forgiving is easier when we have the confidence that we are less likely to be hurt again in the same way.

Trust is for the future.

Because of what had happened in the past, I could not trust my ex in certain situations. I started with an example below. You fill in yours.

"I can't trust that my ex won't... have angry outbursts."

1. _____

2. _____

3. _____

4. _____

5. _____

---

[1] These examples were adapted from Brad Hambrick's "Three Dimensions of Forgiveness," (March 2020).

6. _____

7. _____

8. _____

9. _____

10. _____

Bottom line: **It is possible to forgive them without trusting them.**

"I DON'T WANT TO FEEL THIS WAY, BUT I'M STILL BITTER AND ANGRY!"

I relate to the saying, "Bitterness is anger turned inward." How true is that? The lack of forgiveness leads to bitterness. Are you still finding yourself with a lack of patience? Feeling angry? Looking at others in contempt? Assuming someone around you has ulterior motives or is against you? Oftentimes, those are symptoms of unforgiveness in deeper areas of our lives, spilling over to the guy who's driving too slow in the fast lane in front of us.

There are other motivations to take steps to forgive.

A lack of forgiveness spills over into other relationships. That means it can affect our children, friends, or even our next relationship. Without forgiveness, we leave a chapter of a book open and start a new book without finishing the last. Without complete forgiveness, we are likely to have poor future emotional connections and we're guaranteed incomplete connections.

We don't want to fast-forward 10 years and be a bitter, angry person.

We've all met them. That older man at the coffee shop who grumbles even if you smile and say hello. If we don't forgive, negativity breeds. We want to get negativity out of our lives and be able to move on. The saying is true: "The lack of forgiveness is like drinking poison and hoping the other person dies."

I found it helped me forgive easier if I had some sort of reassurance that I wouldn't be hurt again in the future, so...

3. I created boundaries so I couldn't be hurt as easily in the future.

As we've already discussed, boundaries are key in our healing process. They were the pivotal gateway to overcoming the deepest hurts in my divorce. Like you, I had a list of what my ex had done that hurt or angered me. In response to those, I created new boundaries.

I didn't do it alone, though. My closest friends came up with most of my new boundaries while I was still in the Wake-Up/Shock and Triage/Prioritize stages. I lacked the clarity of thought or any semblance of confidence or courage to come up with ideas of boundaries, which is natural.

Suggested Assignment: Ask one or two close friends to help brainstorm specific boundaries in response to your list of offenses (see pages 46-47). If you're like me, it was hard to come up with them on my own. I was too close to the situation, and friends had perspective I was lacking.

WHY CAN'T I MOVE ON?

We are creatures of habit. We don't know what we don't know, including accepting bad behavior on one or both sides. However, acknowledging and recognizing my fears and the areas I needed to forgive helped me brainstorm ideas of boundaries I could create to avoid further hurt or damage in those same areas in my future. Now you can do that for yourself. I started with an example below. You fill in yours.

My example: I can't trust that my ex won't have angry outbursts, so from now on I will... require text-only contact.

Now, fill in your responses to those situations below by completing the sentence:

"To protect me from putting myself in a position to be hurt or damaged in the future, from now on I will... "

Next, look back at your first list of "I can't trust that my ex won't..." (see pages 46-47)

1. _____

2. _____

3. _____

4. _____

5. _____

6. _____

HOW TO DIVORCE WELL

7. _____

8. _____

9. _____

10. _____

Once I realized that forgiveness was for the past, I realized I was in control of whether it would continue to affect me in the future. It didn't mean the other person would change. It meant I then had control of how I would respond.

I could...

- Remove myself from the situation.
  (I have control over who I allow in my life)
- Change the situation so it didn't have the ability to affect me as much, i.e. I don't need to go to that establishment to eat, or to that church right now, or drive the route that goes right by that location.
- Commit to not re-entering the relationship by taking physical steps (legally, physically, or emotionally) to not be associated with them in the future.

Boundaries helped me create what I called my forgiveness bubble.

As soon as something happened that disregarded or violated my boundaries, I lost forgiveness for him. I felt like he invaded my bubble. My heart would beat really hard, and I would feel the anger well up in me if I sensed my boundaries were even threatened or discounted. But as

WHY CAN'T I MOVE ON?

long as I could keep him outside of my boundaries, I could keep him forgiven.

Here's a little peek into part of my forgiveness bubble.

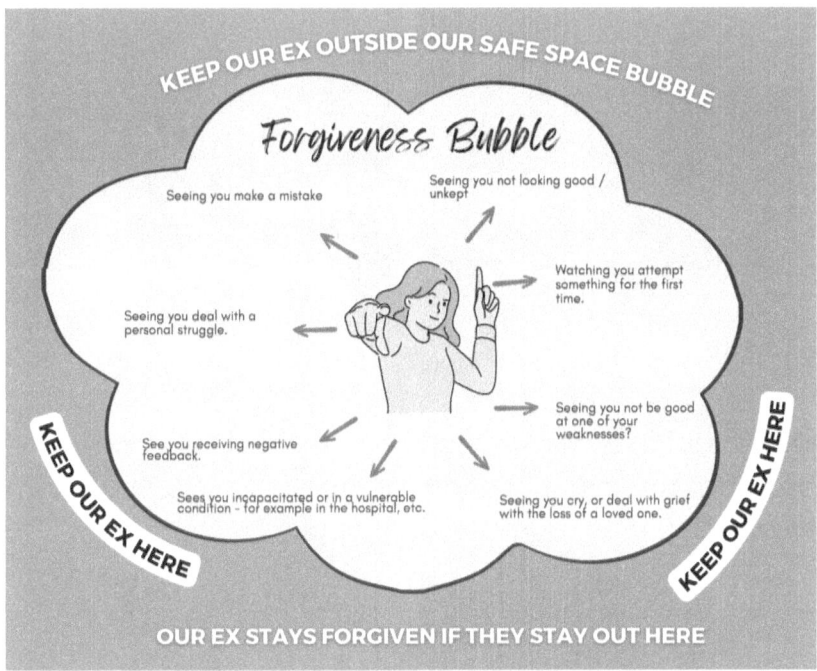

Who was in control of that? Me.

Who is in control of your forgiveness bubble? YOU!

You design your bubble to look exactly like you need it to feel safe and protected.

HOW TO DIVORCE WELL

NOW IT'S YOUR TURN!

What are scenarios that make you feel vulnerable or exposed?

Here's a list of scenarios that made me feel vulnerable and exposed. You might consider your potential experiences in the coming months (circle what applies):

- Sharing a creative work, like art, writing, or music, for the first time.
- Public speaking or giving presentations in front of a large audience.
- Processing the pain associated with the abandonment or pain in the divorce.
- Experiencing a medical examination or procedure.
- Being in a job interview or evaluation.
- Facing criticism or negative feedback.
- Dealing with the loss of a loved one or grieving.
- Seeing you make mistakes or fail.
- Going through financial difficulties and seeking help or support.
- Confronting a phobia, fear, or weakness.

WHY CAN'T I MOVE ON?

To be noted: These situations can vary from person to person, and what makes me feel vulnerable or exposed may not have the same effect on you.

Emotional boundaries are essential for maintaining all of our relationships in a healthy way, and when they are disregarded or violated, it naturally leads to emotional distress and strain. Here are some examples of emotional boundaries being trampled on:

1. Invalidating Your Feelings:
   - Dismissing or belittling your emotions.
   - Telling you that you shouldn't feel a certain way or that your feelings are wrong.
2. Manipulation:
   - Emotional manipulation, such as guilt-tripping or using emotional blackmail.
   - Playing mind games to control or influence your emotions.
3. Lack of Respect for Privacy:
   - Invading your personal space without permission.
   - Reading a personal messages or diary without your consent.
4. Unsolicited Advice:
   - Offering advice without being asked, especially when it's not constructive.
   - Insisting that their solution is the only correct one.
5. Constant Criticism:
   - Regularly pointing out flaws or criticizing your choices.
   - Undermining your self-esteem through constant negative comments.

6. Emotional Dependency:
   - Relying heavily on you for emotional support without reciprocating.
   - Expecting you to meet all of their emotional needs, which creates an unhealthy dynamic.
7. Boundary Violations in Intimate Relationships:
   - Ignoring your request for space or time alone.
   - Pressuring you into intimate activities your are uncomfortable with.
8. Betrayal of Trust:
   - Sharing your personal secrets without your permission.
   - Continue to engage in actions that break your trust, such as infidelity.
9. Emotional Abuse:
   - Name-calling, insults, or demeaning language.
   - Controlling behavior, isolation, or using threats to manipulate emotions.
10. Disregarding Consent:
    - Ignoring your expressed boundaries or crossing physical boundaries without your consent.
    - Pressuring you into situations you are not comfortable with.

Whatever makes you feel vulnerable or exposed, and your ex-spouse witnesses it, it's important to acknowledge and address these feelings when they arise. I found it essential to reach out to trusted friends or even a therapist to cope with them effectively.

We need to recognize and communicate our emotional boundaries. To foster a healthy relationship, your former spouse needs to respect and acknowledge those boundaries. If they don't, we limit access. This is where the Forgiveness

WHY CAN'T I MOVE ON?

Bubble comes in – we limit their accessibility, thus their ability to offend or hurt us.

> We limit their accessibility, thus their ability to offend or hurt us.
> #HowToDivorceWell

Now, given that there is no requirement to trust our ex in the future, is forgiveness an easier pill to swallow? It was for me. Differentiating forgiveness from trust and building boundaries to protect and preserve the future was key.

THEN, I HAD TO EAT MY WORDS

Yes, I forgave initially in words, but then I'd drive by a familiar location and it would instantly bring me back to a scenario with a horrible memory and I would be right back at square one with a boatload of anger. I'd go from calm and cool to mad as FIRE in 0.25 seconds! Can you relate? So, the next step was to recognize forgiveness wasn't a one-and-done proposition. Forgiveness is something hard-fought with an option to do or don't do daily... sometimes hourly, or on a minute-by-minute basis.

WOULD YOU BE WILLING TO TRY SOMETHING, EVEN IF YOU DON'T WANT TO, IF I TELL YOU IT WORKS?

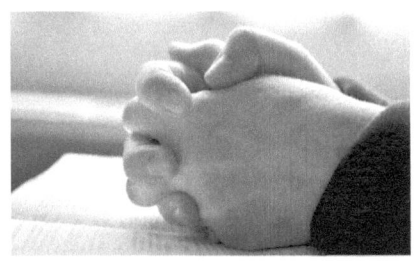

"Bless those who curse you, pray for those who mistreat you." Luke 6:28

HOW TO DIVORCE WELL

Journey with me on this one... I wondered why the Bible says, "Bless those who curse you, pray for those who mistreat you." Fine, I can forgive them, but BLESS them? Seriously? Yes, pray for those who hurt you. Why? It works!

Three things to consider, and how they could look in divorce:

- Pray for our enemies – "God help me to forgive Jim."
- Bless our enemies – "I pray he is a good dad to the kids this weekend."
- Do good to your enemies – "I commit to saying something kind about my ex to my kids."

I'm not suggesting you bless them and pray for them because it's the "right" thing to do, even if it is, I'm asking you to do it because the anger, resentment and even hurt will subside. This isn't about them deserving the forgiveness, it is about YOU deserving the freedom to move forward and creating a new life for you to thrive.

> This isn't about them deserving the forgiveness, it is about YOU deserving the freedom to move forward and creating a new life for you to thrive.
> #HowToDivorceWell

Many clients have been helped by this version of the Resentment Prayer (author unknown)

This is the prayer:

Prayer For Freedom from Resentment

God,
(insert name), like me, is an imperfect person.

Please:
- Help me to show (insert name) tolerance, compassion, and patience;
- Release me from being angry;
- Enable me to release this resentment;
- Remove this resentment;
- Show me how to take a kindly and tolerant view of (insert name);
- Bring me to accept reality as it is; and
- Show me how I can be helpful to (insert name).

Your will be done.
Amen

GIVE YOURSELF A BREAK! THERE'S A REASON IT'S HARD TO FORGIVE THEM...

- You may have trusted an untrustworthy person. That's not your fault.
  I had to ask myself: Can I forgive them anyway?

- You may have been left with less than what you walked into the relationship with.
  I had to ask myself: Can I forgive them anyway?
  I can rebuild again.

- You may have lasting scars that cannot be undone. I had to ask myself: Can I forgive them anyway? Those scars will be used for your story. You can decide now if it will be used for good or bad. The wounds may hurt now, if you heal and scar well, you will build a foundation for you to help others who are where you are now. The more you hurt, the more powerful and effective your story will be to help others.

When the answer is eventually yes to all the preceding questions, you are close to freedom from what can be referred to as "baggage" going into the next chapter of your life.

FAST-TRACK STRATEGY:

Here is a trick: Praying for them the moment a bad memory or resentment pops into our minds is a fast-track key to healing and moving forward faster. Consider it a "prayer trigger" that leads us one step closer to freedom each time.

For example, Jim was late to pick up the kids AGAIN! "God, I pray Jim is a good dad to the kids this weekend."

IT'S TOO HARD TO FORGIVE!

Yep. It is. It is hard, but I believe it's worth it. Not only because it's better for us to heal, but because the lack of forgiveness can get us into a lot of trouble. It can cause us to live in anger. That can be dangerous.

WHY CAN'T I MOVE ON?

This is a perfect illustration of the quote:

"Don't be quick to fly off the handle. Anger boomerangs. You can spot a fool by the lumps on his head."
(Ecclesiastes 7:9 MSG)

Karen Swartz from the Johns Hopkins Medical Group states that research has indicated that forgiveness relieves stress and lowers blood pressure. In addition, further research concludes in many cases it can also increase immunity, relieve nightmares, insomnia, angry outbursts, emotional numbness, and physical and emotional tension. Are you experiencing any of that? I sure was.

A client of my divorce coaching course, who is not particularly religious, explained this to me:

"When you told me to pray for my ex because I was so angry and hurt, I was having a hard time moving forward. In fact, he was already remarried when I finally realized I still hadn't forgiven my ex. He still affected my life, yet he was living a new life – footloose and fancy-free. It wasn't fair and that angered me even worse.

You asked me to pray, and you know I am not a very religious person. It was too difficult to pray. I needed another option until I could possibly pray for him. I was relieved that it didn't mean I was stuck just because I was not wanting to talk to God about him. I was actually still mad at God for letting this all happen. You helped me come up with my own phrase that I said over and over again when I was obsessing about him, angry, hurt, sad or bitter. It was a way of retraining my brain. This was mine:

I forgive (my ex) because we were both broken people. I forgive myself, and I forgive him. I look forward to the freedom I get from forgiveness as I move forward.

YOUR CHOICE – DO WANT YOUR EX TO CONTROL YOU?

In the middle of my divorce, I was given a daily devotional, "Every Day in His Presence," written by one of my favorite pastors, Dr. Charles Stanley. When urging us to forgive he says,

"You may be tempted to stop reading because confronting unresolved anger is painful. But realize, unforgiveness can damage your health, thwart your peace, hinder your joy, and harm your relationships. Bitterness prevents you from living the abundant life God created you to enjoy. And **as long as you refuse to forgive the offender, you allow him or her to control you.**

Friend, don't allow resentment to imprison you. Release your anger to the Lord and trust Him to heal you. The Father knows what's happened and He judges the situation with wisdom and righteousness. So let go of the pain, forgive, and trust Him to vindicate you. Then allow Him to heal your heart as only He can.

> Pray, 'Lord, please help me forgive. Heal me of this bitterness and show me how to live in Your freedom. Amen.'"

Want a better future?

How many of us know people who have not taken the time to heal after a divorce, but instead have ended up dating, marrying, and then divorcing again soon after? If we don't go through the healing, we can keep resentments, hurt, pain, anger, defense systems, and denial.

Just because we're dating a new person, will those things just magically disappear? No. We can end up going into a new relationship with those same unresolved feelings (also known as "baggage"). Is that fair to us or the person we're dating? I think we can all agree it's not. If we're honest with ourselves, it's selfish. We're filling a void to feel better because divorce hurts.

BUT WHAT IF I CAN'T CONTACT MY EX TO FORGIVE THEM?

"It's not safe physically or emotionally to talk with them."
"But what if they passed away?"
"But what if there's no way to get in contact with them?"

We don't need to talk to them directly.

- We can write a letter and burn it (like I did).
- We can write it on a note, put it in a balloon and release it.
- We can even read it at their gravesite.

The key is YOU, not them. The key is the action – not the feeling – of forgiveness.

> Don't treat people as bad as they are; treat them as good as you are.

"I BELIEVE IN PRAYER, BUT IT'S TOO HARD TO PRAY FOR MY EX"

Prayer is the key. I get it. When I didn't want to forgive, I had to *pray for the willingness to be willing* to forgive them. Really. It sounds crazy, but God will and does remove those barriers. It may not happen quickly, but it does happen eventually.

What does that look like for you?

"God, Give me the willingness to be willing to forgive _____."

One day it will feel okay to say, "God give me the willingness to forgive _____."

And one day, without any big announcement from the sky, you will suddenly be able to say, "God, as much as I forgive myself, and know Your forgiveness, I also forgive _____. Please help me have forgiveness in my heart right now."

Remember – it's not a feeling. It's an action.

BUT WHAT IF...

> My ex is continuing with the behavior that hurt me in the marriage?
> What my ex did has a lasting impact and they've left me with a horrible disease?
> My ex left me with an unwanted pregnancy?
> My ex left me in financial ruin?

We can forgive them for the action. We can release them from retribution. We can leave that for God. Throughout the Bible, it tells stories of how God repays. "'Vengeance is mine,' says the Lord," and "God repays all the wickedness."

Then, borrow my favorite prayer:

"God, sic' em!"

Don't misunderstand: Offering our ex complete forgiveness doesn't mean we don't divorce. It doesn't mean they don't pay for their part. It doesn't mean that they don't

"God, sic' em!"
#HowToDivorceWell

have responsibility for their actions. It always helps me to remember forgiveness is not the same thing as trust. I don't need to trust my ex anymore.

NEED TO FORGIVE GOD?

"God, why are you allowing this to happen to me?"
"I was doing right. How can You be a 'good Father' and allow this to happen?"

To forgive God, I had to step back and take an aerial view of my situation. I ultimately had to find a bigger meaning in the whole process. That's what pushed me to write this book. I kept praying, "God, don't let my pain be in vain." I don't pretend to understand all the ways and the whys of God. I know there is a bigger picture – always. We may not be able to change our circumstances, but I found we *can* use our story to affect the future and help others in their journeys as we get to the other side.

Anyone want a sneak peek into my dream?

One day, you link arms with me and others as we create a community of HOW TO DIVORCE WELL HEROES. Our stories will inspire others who are behind us. Yours already is. There's someone who isn't as far along as you are now, and they are watching *you*. Unfortunately, we are not likely the last men and women to get divorced. One day, you will be able to reach out to the next person in pain. You may not believe me now, but if you keep putting the work in, you will get out of this pain. I promise. A new, exciting life is waiting for you. If you can't quite believe that yet, I'll believe it for you until you can! Your unique story will one day be able to give strength and courage to others who are in the middle of their pain. I can't wait! But I'm getting ahead of myself... for now.

LET'S FOCUS ON YOU AND PUT IT TO WORK!

What are three things you wish you could've done better? Or, consider three things you'll do differently if you enter into a new relationship.

1. _____

2. _____

3. _____

THE HARDEST ONE TO FORGIVE

Here's the tough one: Have you forgiven yourself? How do you forgive yourself? That's been the hardest one for me. Did you make any mistakes in your marriage? I certainly did. I've had to write those things out and literally forgive myself for them. I had to take responsibility for my part, and I had to remember that forgiveness is an action. The way to live a life that I'm proud of going forward is to make reparations to those I hurt and forgive myself in the process.

But then every once in a while, a memory would pop into my mind, and I'd cringe. Maybe it was guilt? Shame? I'm not sure. But in that moment, I wish I could've gone back and changed my actions or what I said. Then I had to ask myself, had I forgiven myself?

God promises us only peace for today.

> 2 Corinthians 3:17 says, "Now the Lord is the Spirit, and where the Spirit of the Lord is, there is freedom."

Do you have shame about anything you did wrong or hurt your kids, like I did?
Does it say, "... where the Spirit of the Lord is, there **was** freedom?" Nope. But often when I was alone with my thoughts, I was flooded with negative talk to myself filled with shame, blame and guilt. I wasn't living in peace for the past.

If I asked for forgiveness of those things in the past, God has already forgotten it, "as far as the East is from the West." (Psalm 103:12) Why do I have to keep beating myself up in my mind? It chipped away at my confidence to think I was able to move forward because I didn't deserve it, would do it wrong again, or I wasn't competent.

Is that God shaming me for the past? No. But why could I not forgive myself?

Truth is, I figured out it was a twisted version of pride in me. Maybe some people call it "false pride."

Pride is when we feel good about sharing an accomplishment. False pride prevented me from accepting my humanity and inherent imperfections, which perpetuated a cycle of self-criticism and prevented my growth and healing.

So, could I forgive myself?

When I thought about it, I began to realize: Who do I think I am that my forgiveness of myself somehow overrode or was more important than God's forgiveness of me?

It does say, "...where the Spirit of the Lord is, there **IS** freedom." He only promises us enough peace for today, right now, at this moment. If we forgive ourselves, we can be promised peace and freedom for today.

Back when I initially realized the wrong I did, THAT'S when the lack of peace happened. THAT'S when I felt guilt. THAT'S when I felt shame. THAT'S when I wished I could go back and change what I had done. Can you relate?

Before I ask you to write those same three things in your list below, let me show you an example of a client's answers:

HOW TO DIVORCE WELL

1. I forgive myself for being naïve.

2. I forgive myself for avoiding confrontation and not addressing him watching porn.

3. I forgive myself for my fear of being alone the rest of my life causing me to not act.

LET'S PUT IT TO WORK:

1. I forgive myself for

_____

2. I forgive myself for

_____

3. I forgive myself for

_____

Great job! Now, before we move on, let's try to retrain our brains to tell ourselves new messages. What do I mean by that? My client needed to know she was not naïve in all situations, and that she could grow to become more perceptive, knowing, educated, enlightened, experienced, knowledgeable, sophisticated, discerning, and insightful. In addition to her daily affirmations (see previous chapter), I had her write out the opposite of the things she needed to forgive herself for.

WHY CAN'T I MOVE ON?

I forgive myself for:	Affirmations:
Making decision to marry him without listening to counsel of people around me.	I am an experienced, mature adult
I was afraid to leave because I don't want to be alone.	I'm a courageous risk taker
I was naïve	Although I see the best in people, and am not a suspicious person, I am a confident woman and can address uncomfortable topics

She added these to her daily affirmations:

1. Although I see the best in people, and am not a suspicious person, I am a confident woman and can address uncomfortable topics.
2. I am an experienced, mature adult.
3. I'm a courageous risk taker.

I encouraged her to look up antonyms for her personal characteristics. FYI: She added those to her daily affirmations and said them for a long time before she believed them.

Now it's your turn to add some affirmations:

1. I am _____

2. I am _____

3. I am _____

Create a prayer card

What are three things your ex left you with that are the hardest to forgive?

1. My ex _____

2. My ex _____

3. My ex _____

Remember the prayer Dr. Stanley suggested? Write out a prayer card and add the three items you just listed. For example:

Write "God, please help me forgive my ex for:

1. _____,

2. _____, and

3. _____.

Heal me of this bitterness and show me how to live in Your freedom. Amen."

WHY CAN'T I MOVE ON?

What are three character traits you won't accept in your next relationship due to your new boundaries? (For example, "I will not tolerate angry outbursts.")

1. I will not accept _____

2. I will not accept _____

3. I will not accept _____

What are some triggers that have brought back cringe-worthy memories? This could be places you've driven by, people who may have called, or posts you've seen on social media.

1. Location _____

2. Location _____

3. Location _____

Keep this last list to look back on for the chapter "This HURTS! Cut it out!"

Now, repeat after me, "I no longer associate my ability to heal with someone else's choices that I have no control over."

Good. Now, what do we do when we're at our absolute wit's end? That's what we cover in the next chapter.

CHAPTER 4

WHO CAN I TRUST?

*"A man of many companions may come to ruin,
but there is a friend who sticks closer than a brother."*
(Proverbs 18:24 ESV)

During this tumultuous time, are there days you just want to get angry and scream, cuss and cry?

- Do you feel wronged?
- Do you feel like people are hearing only one side of the story and they don't hear your side?
- Do you need to vent?
- Are you feeling too vulnerable from your personal life being laid out for the world to see?
- Are you sharing your anger and justifications with your kids?
- Do you feel unjustly accused?

- Are you feeling weak and like you don't know what to do at certain times?
- Are you in shock and still triaging and have a case of brain fog?
- Are you finding yourself saying or doing things to people that you later regret?
- Are you isolating?

I FOUND A SOLUTION

I was concerned that the details of my personal life were being exposed. I felt misunderstood. I felt alone... very alone. I felt like everyone in my social circle knew my personal business. I knew people were gossiping, and I was hearing through the grapevine what people were saying. I found myself dealing with problems in my work that otherwise wouldn't have been an issue had my personal life not been known at my company. I found I was isolating and spiraling in negativity.

I quickly thought of how my dad dealt with his divorce.

My dad reached out to his brother regularly, and he brought a couple of close friends into his inner circle to know all the details and struggles during the divorce. When anyone outside would ask how he was doing, he would politely tell them he's fine. He was implementing his life principle of living in his concentric circles (which I will explain later in this chapter).

I thought he was fine. That's what he showed me, and that's what I heard him tell others. Turns out, he later told me he was not fine. He was heartbroken, mad, and felt incredibly ashamed to be divorcing. I would've never known. I was shocked when, in my 20s, he told me the extent of his experience.

He asked, "Don't you remember going grocery shopping with me and telling me what I needed to buy?" I just thought it was fun going to the grocery store with my dad. I didn't think of it as Dad not knowing something. He also reminded me of the time he put water in a pan and the entire soup can – yes, the can itself – into the pot of water. I thought that was funny given I was about seven years old at the time. I didn't mind helping Dad. I thought it was kind of cool. It didn't even cross my mind to think of him as anything other than capable.

So as a child, Dad didn't share with me the extent to which he was mad and ashamed. After all, it wasn't something an adult would share with a child. However, it wasn't just me he didn't share with. I never even heard him discuss anything negative about the divorce with another adult when he was interacting with family and friends. He was calm, cool, and collected. I thought he had it all together.

Fast-forward 30 years, and I found myself getting divorced.

I realized I needed to do what my dad had done. However, I was not calm, cool, and collected. I went back and forth from isolating in a pool of fear and self-pity to cussing, crying, and screaming, and not caring who heard. Thankfully, I had three people in my inner circle who were there to absorb the dark side of the hardest days.

Having watched how my dad had processed through divorce, I knew I needed to be a better person and develop

HOW TO DIVORCE WELL

my key support group. The principle Dad followed was what Moses did when he needed help to win a war. He counted on Aaron and Hur:

> "Aaron and Hur held up Moses' arms during the Israelites' battle against the Amalekites. When the Amalekites attacked the Israelites on their way to the Promised Land, Moses stood on a hill overlooking the battle, staff in hand, and raised his arms in a position of prayer (Exodus 17:8–9). As long as Moses' arms were raised, the Israelites prevailed, but, when he lowered his hands, the Amalekites began to overtake the Israelites (verse 11). **So, when Moses' arms grew tired**, he sat on a stone and **Aaron and Hur stood beside him to hold up his arms**. Due to Aaron and Hur's support, **"[Moses'] hands remained steady** till sunset. So, Joshua overcame the Amalekite army with the sword."[2]
> (Exodus 17:12–13)

WHO ARE YOUR AARON AND HUR?

Do you have a close friend? Someone you can scream in anger about your situation to and they will give you a big emotional hug and tell you that everything's going to be okay? Write that person's name down. Now, think about the last moment you were in distress, exasperated or enraged about something – anything. Other than that close friend, who did you share your experience with?

---

[2] As described by GotQuestions.org

WHO CAN I TRUST?

Now, go through your phone to look at contacts if you want to and write down names of others who feel like "safe" people.

_____ _____ _____

_____ _____ _____

_____ _____ _____

Now go back to your list and put a check mark next to two more people in your life who would take your phone call at 3am and let you cuss, cry and scream, and still love you in the morning. Those are your **3-at-3**.

> 3 people you can call at 3am and cuss, cry or scream and they'll still love you in the morning. Those are your 3-at-3
> #HowToDivorceWell

WHY 3-AT-3?

Often, the chaos of losing your marriage and all the aspects surrounding it can cause us to make decisions and tell people things we later regret. For instance, here's my friend's story, who "over shared" (in her words) and came to later regret it.

"My ex-husband had done us so wrong, and if I'm being truthful to myself, I wanted everyone to know. He left us. He hired his big-money attorneys, and the kids and I were left without a voice or a way to be heard. I needed help. In one particular moment of despair, I posted on Facebook my side of the story and told people I needed help. I also shared that divorce is terrible, and my feelings of abandonment. It was how I really felt, and at the time, it felt cathartic to get it out. I didn't think of the ramifications of posting it.

Two of my Facebook posts were used as evidence in our divorce court case. I was mortified! The divorce was bad enough. At that very moment, I realized I had done something *after* my ex left that made it even worse for us!

The hardest moment was when I realized what I had inadvertently done to my kids. Although I felt like I was reaching out for help for us, and I had good motives, What I didn't realize was their friends and their friends' parents would see the posts. My kids were forced to engage in conversations at school about our divorce. How were they supposed to answer questions from well-meaning parents? They hadn't even been able to heal on their own before they were having to field questions they didn't have the maturity or full story to answer. Even the well-minded families who took pity on us and talked to my kids about divorce made my kids feel uncomfortable.

I really wish I would've kept my mouth shut and been satisfied to just confide in a friend. I really blew it." – R

WHO CAN I TRUST?

Doesn't your heart break for her? Yeah, I wish she would've reached out to me earlier, too. It was just gut wrenching to watch the fallout unfold in her ensuing court case (which was when she finally reached out to me).

As a friend, what would you have done?

If my client above who "really blew it" was a close friend of yours, and you saw one of her social media posts, how would you have responded? Would you have ignored it? Would you have thought, "She's just processing, she'll be okay." Or would you have picked up the phone immediately and said, "WHAT THE HECK ARE YOU THINKING? TAKE THAT POST DOWN!" (Or in slightly nicer terms but gotten the point across.)

I think we all can agree she would have benefitted from having a 3-at-3. Even if she posted something on social media, one of her 3-at-3 likely would've quickly called her and talked her through the potential ramifications of her posts. One of them likely would've helped her think it through and possibly even convinced her to take it down before it had the opportunity to have such catastrophic implications.

> *"By yourself you're unprotected.*
> *With a friend you can face the worst.*
> *Can you round up a third?*
> *A three-stranded rope isn't easily snapped."*
> (Ecclesiastes 4:9-12 MSG)

"WHAT'S THE BIG DEAL ABOUT POSTING ON SOCIAL MEDIA?"

Ready for an eye-opening fact? Facebook is the number one source for online divorce evidence. In fact, studies show 81% of AAML divorce attorneys have used or encountered evidence obtained from social media.[3]

I've learned it's wise to keep all issues related to the relationship off social media. Why give ammunition to our ex's attorney? Afterall, people who care about you want to hear about you in a personal conversation – not on social media.

So, as you go through this process, the key to the 3-at-3 is getting through the critical days – the first year or first year and a half. You don't want an unmanageable number of people knowing everything. Truth is, it's exhausting to process your emotions with a lot of people. You need to conserve your emotional energy for your priorities. Your precious energy is needed to keep you moving forward into your successful future.

People didn't know when I got divorced.

From the day of writing this book, it has been four years since we separated and two years since the divorce was final. I just announced on Facebook and Instagram that I'm writing a book about divorce. I have had countless people respond to me saying they were shocked I was divorced. Although it was obvious to some with the lack of photos together, it wasn't to everyone.

---

[3] American Academy of Matrimonial Lawyers (AAML) Feb 10, 2010, 12:19 ET

WHO CAN I TRUST?

Why is that? I do not put the negative side of my personal life on Facebook. That is my goal. When I get angry, it does not go on social media.

Do negative things happen? Yes. Is it any less valid if it's not on Facebook? No.

Have I typed things in and deleted them? Yes. I think we've all done that. It is a muscle of self-control that we all need to develop during this time. Type it in. Delete it.

Write the letter to your ex, burn it, or put it away in the back of a drawer. They don't need to see it until one of your 3-at-3 gets to read over it or think through it with you. You can send it after you have received some sound advice and slept on it. You can do this!

Are you open to remarrying one day?

Afterall, if we're open to the idea of remarrying or dating again one day, we need to consider if we want our future spouse to look at what we're posting today. We need to think long-term – 5, 10, or 15 years down the road. This is a key component of how to divorce well. It means being comfortable with not sharing our side of the story right now. What we share today can hurt us tomorrow.

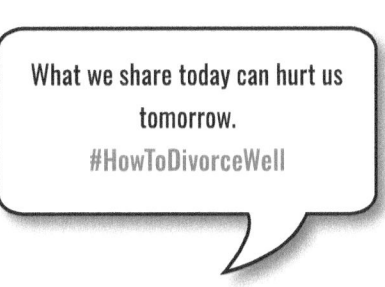
What we share today can hurt us tomorrow.
#HowToDivorceWell

"I HAVE SO MANY DECISIONS TO MAKE AND I DON'T KNOW WHERE TO START!"

The Bible talks about there being, "wisdom in a multitude of counselors." We're not made to live as isolated, emotional islands. We're not made to go through pain and rebuilding alone. When I was broken, empty, scared, vulnerable, and felt completely defeated, those 3-at-3 would help think for me.

For the first two years, I could not think straight. There were many decisions I needed to make when I would call or text my 3-at-3 and ask, "What do I say?" or "What do I do?" I did not trust my own responses.

I was so emotional and so completely devastated; I was caught between feeling like a helpless victim and an angry warrior. I was reactionary and when I needed to make a decision or my ex would do something horrible (like call me), my heart would beat a thousand miles a minute. Especially with decisions in the very beginning, even if I had a hunch of what to do, I would run it by one of my 3-at-3 first.

> I was caught between feeling like a helpless victim and an angry warrior.
> #HowToDivorceWell

They always provided fresh perspectives on my dilemmas, helping me solve problems in new ways. Oftentimes, they would just give me encouragement and affirmation, and other times, they would suggest to wait when I was reacting. Just taking the time to text or call those three would help me process. The simple action of typing it out functioned

WHO CAN I TRUST?

as a means of give me space to think more clearly about potential options and ideas.

When one of them would say, "Yes, you can do it. Go ahead and send that text," or "Go ahead and respond to this financial situation," I had greater confidence. In some situations, I would only need to hear back from one of them, and I could make the decision or take the necessary action.

Other times, I needed all three of them, with one sitting beside me as I tackled a difficult task, wrote a text, or composed a document. In the beginning, I needed courage and support to have difficult conversations. I had a hard time saying what I needed to say on the phone, via email or text to my ex. They held me accountable to boundaries and kept me from either losing my temper, buckling in fear, or getting too emotional when I needed to be reasonable.

> What I really felt like doing was screaming cuss words at him and calling him every name in the book
> #HowToDivorceWell

What I really felt like doing was screaming cuss words at him and calling him every name in the book (and I'm not a person who generally cusses). Hmmm... thank goodness my 3-at-3 didn't hold me to that high character bar during those hard years. I completely blew any sainthood trait out of the water!

"I FEEL SO WEAK AND ALONE!"

This is what I found: Your 3-at-3 will have confidence for you when you don't have confidence in yourself. They know you well and they will help you make decisions as if you were

HOW TO DIVORCE WELL

acting as the best version of yourself with **your** best interest in mind. My 3-at-3 were my backbone when I didn't have one, and they were providing my backbone for God to fill until I had my own again.

Another friend shared her regret of giving too many details to a work associate who happened to be in management:

> "Years ago, I helped a girlfriend get her current job where I work. We are good friends, but I didn't consider what would happen when I shared what was happening in my marriage with her. In the middle of my divorce, I was in a tough spot and was looking to make a career change.
>
> I asked her for a letter of recommendation for a new position in our company. She said she would keep me in mind, but also said, 'it might not be a great time for you to hold a position that requires a lot of emotional energy, as you're already dealing with a lot in your personal life.' What? Who was she to decide what I could and couldn't deal with? I regretted ever telling her about the problems in my marriage. I had no idea it would come back to bite me (in the butt)!"

Have good friends at work? That can be helpful as they can cover for you or build you up when you're feeling down. A few words to the wise about who you share with at work:

- Is the work associate able to use the information to hurt you in any way?
- Is the work associate in a position to affect decisions regarding the future of your employment?

HOW DO YOU CONNECT WITH YOUR 3-AT-3?

I made it simple. When I had a question or a situation that I was fired up about, I texted one of my 3-at-3 and then copied and pasted that message separately to the other two. No one is going to be available all the time, but chances are at least one of those three friends is going to be able to respond to you.

DO THEY KNOW THEY'RE YOUR 3-AT-3?

Does it need to be a formal invitation? Let's consider what happened to one of my clients before we had connected:

> "I have a close group of girlfriends who are all in a text thread together. At one of the many parties we attend together, one of the ladies pulled me aside to share with me a suggestion for a financial issue I was dealing with in my separation. I knew I hadn't told her about it. It turns out, the friend I had talked to about it, shared it with her in hopes of finding suggestions to my financial conundrum. I felt like my personal life was exposed – I felt my trust had been violated. I love both of these women, and I know it was done with the best of intentions, but I didn't necessarily want to share that with everyone."

It's been said, "A secret can be either too good to keep, or not good enough to keep."

Another client had a similar situation, but it was a group of friends who were couples. He ran into a similar problem.

HOW TO DIVORCE WELL

"My former wife and I were part of a dinner party group. Many of the men golfed together and as couples we would often travel together. One day on the golf course I was letting off some steam about my ex-wife. She was making it so hard for me to see my kids that morning, and I remember being furious. I guess I was telling the guys because I just needed to vent. I was pissed.

Later that next week, my ex started out a conversation about our kids with, "I know you think I'm making it hard to see the kids..." How would she know that? I realized it had gone from one of the guys to their wife, and to my ex. Now I was really pissed."

In both scenarios I would imagine my clients were feeling a sense of betrayal, maybe even feeling exposed. What if both of my clients had a defining conversation with their friends saying, "Joe, there are things I'm wanting to share with you that only you will know. Would I be able to trust that if I reach out for your input or even just want to blow off some steam, it would be kept strictly between you and me?"

After identifying who you know deep in your heart that if you called them in an absolute crisis emergency at 3am, they would answer and they would help you, it's wise to have that conversation with them. Hit on these points:

- You're the only one who might know a lot of what I tell you.
- I have two other friends who I'm talking to, and that's it.
- Can I trust you to keep it between us?

WHO CAN I TRUST?

FYI: Truth be told, I never had to call any of my 3-at-3 at 3am, but knowing that I _could_ helped me in those deep, dark, scary times when I woke up in complete fear. I could at least text or voice message them, knowing they would read/listen to my text in the morning. That was often enough to lessen my anxiety and allow me to go back to sleep.

One of my 3-at-3 had young kids at the time. I asked if she would be willing to turn her ringer off when she went to bed. I could then text her in the middle of the night when I woke up at 3am, but she wouldn't have to read it until the next morning. That worked great for us.

Keep in mind that every member of your 3-at-3 will not have all the qualities you need. One might be a spiritual advisor. One might be great with emotional issues, like a counselor. One will have insight or business sense and can help you financially. They all don't need to have the same qualities, but they do need to be trustworthy and people you know you can tell anything to or be vulnerable and transparent with. We need guidance from a trusted, clear-headed person at that time.

WHAT IF I DON'T HAVE THREE CLOSE FRIENDS I TRULY TRUST?

You're not alone. Many don't. That's okay. You can still benefit from the three you will need by using what my dad explained to me as his concentric circles. There is not just one circle of friends. My dad drew it out, and he had a series of multiple circles outside of his inner circle which represented his inner circle of friends.

HOW TO DIVORCE WELL

Let me explain what I call my dad's concentric circles.

DAD'S CONCENTRIC CIRCLES

When I was about 13, I remember the day my dad took me out to breakfast and described his circles of friends. He was teaching it to me in hopes it would guide me through a difficult situation at the time. He used the example of the divorce to explain how he navigated that very challenging experience. He said he had three who were in his inner circle at the time - his brother, and two fellow pilot friends.

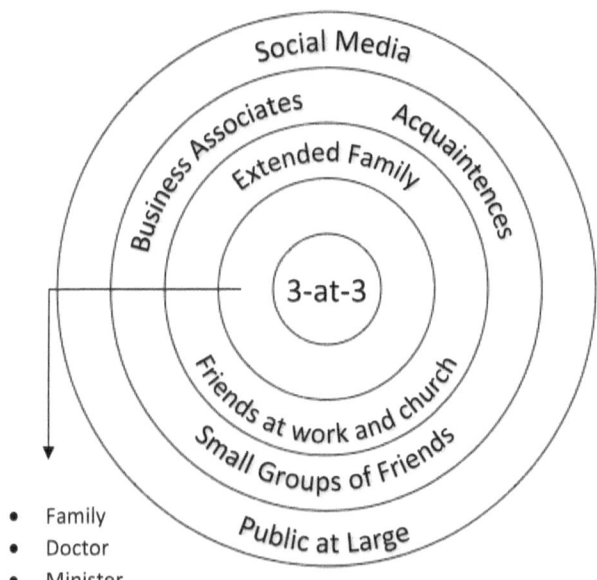

Dad's Concentric Circles

- Family
- Doctor
- Minister
- Attorney
- Divorce Coach
- Therapist / Counselor
- Accountant / Financial Advisor

WHO CAN I TRUST?

Later in life, I was in the middle with his new wife and brother, my Uncle Joe. That was it. He just had the three of us there. Outside of that circle was a fraternity that he was a part of. He was a commercial airline pilot and he said although most pilots shared a lot of information about their personal lives while chatting in the cockpit, he normally didn't. He kept business and personal relationships separate. That served him very well in his divorce. The people who helped him through it were family and his fraternity. The further coworkers, friends and acquaintances were from his inner circles, the less personal information he would divulge.

Now, if Dad would have been social media savvy, the very, very outside of the sixth layer of concentric circles would be any type of social media platform.

If a certain situation arises, and you can stand firm and wait for one of your 3-at-3 to respond to you, you will thank yourself later.

I'm not patient. I work on it, but it's something that creeps into every area of my life. Some of the worst decisions I've made can be traced back to decisions I've made which could've been avoided had I waited.

I learned the hard way

When I got impatient or emotional, I shared a few details with a couple of people I later regretted telling. One was my hair stylist, and one was my nail lady. It sure felt cathartic in the moment, but in my following visits when they'd ask about that specific issue, I didn't feel as comfortable disclosing all of those details (and honestly couldn't believe I had in the

HOW TO DIVORCE WELL

first place!). In one of the instances I didn't even remember having told her anything that vulnerable.

Learn from my mistakes

Try not to give information to people that you don't know really well, you can really trust, or individuals who may not have your best interest in mind. Wait for your 3-at-3 to respond to you. If they don't, go to your next circle with your issue. When I did go outside of my first two circles, I deeply regretted it. You'll avoid a lot of pain and regret by keeping vulnerable or negative topics within your closest circle.

I had one of my 3-at-3 tell me, "I don't want you to take my listening to your anger as my tacit agreement when it doesn't always mean that. It means I'll let you vent your frustration and anger, but I'm not always sure I want you to take any action based on what you're saying. 'Anger of man never accomplishes the righteousness that God requires.'"

I didn't want to hear that, but she was right. God does not want us to act out of our anger. There are times we do have anger, but when we operate out of it without wisdom, it can be ruinous. Run it by one of your 3-at-3. They're likely able to help you temper that anger. I needed to hear that as it gave me permission to be angry, cuss, cry, and scream, but know that it wasn't going any further.

WHO CAN I TRUST?

LET'S PUT IT TO WORK:

Who are the people you run into daily that you need to tell minimal information to at work or in your daily life:

_____ _____ _____

_____ _____ _____

_____ _____ _____

_____ _____ _____

_____ _____ _____

_____ _____ _____

_____ _____ _____

Get it? This list should be long.
You'll thank yourself later.

YOUR SECOND CIRCLE

Some people who are specialists in areas of need during divorce, (attorney, financial consultant, doctor, etc), may currently be strangers, but might ultimately learn more about your divorce than family members.

I would've never expected at the beginning of this process that certain people would end up knowing a whole lot more about my personal life than most of my friends and family. I had to be okay with that. It ultimately felt good. I felt protected. I felt like I was in a safe bubble. I was controlling the information flow.

Now, identify people who are friends, or friends of friends, who can help you in the following areas:

Divorce Attorney: _____
Counselor/Therapist: _____
Health Coach Friend: _____
Divorce Coach: _____
Financial Advisor: _____
Spiritual Friend: _____

These people may not qualify as your 3-at-3, but they are the next layer in your circle during this time – your second circle. Now, to fill these positions, you may need a referral. It may be a friend of a friend or a stranger.

Let's do it:

- Look back at your first list of people.
- Next look at those listed for your second circle above.
- Consider what your personal qualifications are for your 3-at-3 and decide who you would list as your 3-at-3?

YOUR 3-AT-3

1. _____

2. _____

3. _____

Homework

Set down the book and call them now. Tell them what you're thinking. Ask them if they could help you have self-control and keep yourself from sharing things with people that you'll later regret. Some you may not even need to ask. They're already in place, but it might be a good idea to let them know they are the only ones who you'll be sharing certain issues with. I found it opened up a dialog to bring our friendships to an even deeper level because they knew they were deeply trusted.

Now you have the opportunity. You're currently controlling the information flow, and you're highly focused on your goal to divorce well, to get to the other side and live your successful life.

HOW TO DIVORCE WELL

Now it's time to fill in your concentric circles. Add names. It helps. (See page 88 for example)

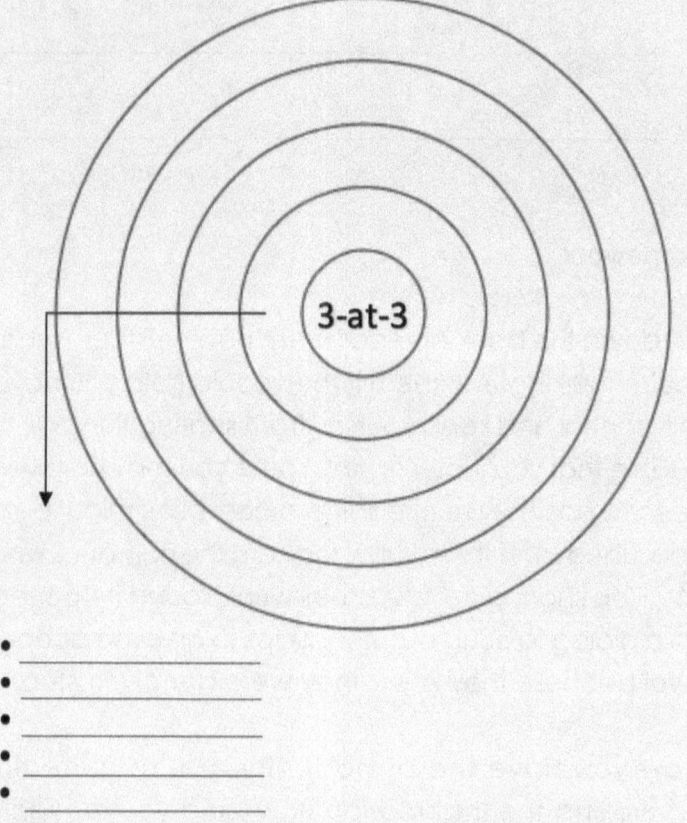

- _____
- _____
- _____
- _____
- _____

Even when we don't tell everyone our side of the story, we can trust that the truth always comes out in the end.

"Someone please tell me I won't always be this angry." You won't. But to help yourself along with that, keep reading.

CHAPTER 5

THIS HURTS! CUT IT OUT!

"I didn't want to move out of hell. I knew all the names of the streets."
Neil Gaiman, *The Sandman*

> "When I'm alone, my thoughts just race with the 'what ifs' and fears. Turning on the TV at least helps me turn off my brain."
>
> "I'm depressed. I know my own negative self-talk is keeping me in a downward spiral."
>
> "I'm hurting. I have another friend who has just been through a bitter divorce, and I don't feel like I can handle all of her drama right now, especially on top of mine... but I feel bad not being there for her as a friend."

Have you ever been around someone who has been eating a lot of garlic and onions? Everyone that gets close to them can tell what they've just eaten because they stink. We are no different. When we allow our minds to be fed with bitterness, doubt, fear, anger, worry, depression, and sarcasm, the people around us can tell what we've been feeding ourselves. Our attitudes stink.

SO, LET'S TALK ABOUT INPUT: Friends

When you hear the terms, "self-focused, negative, and self-absorbed," who comes to mind? Are there people in your circle those who want to bad-mouth their ex as their way to commiserate with you? Maybe someone who talks about their new ailments each time you speak? What about a family member who wants to gossip or talk about an offense with another family member?

THIS HURTS! CUT IT OUT!

What friends, associates or family members come to mind?

_____   _____

_____   _____

_____   _____

Now, consider where you are emotionally. Would you say you're already emotionally, mentally, and physically drained during this process? The answer is probably, "Yes." The following explained why to me:

> "A troublemaker plants seeds of strife;
> gossip separates the best of friends."
> (Prov. 16:28 NLT)

SO, LET'S TALK ABOUT INPUT: Television/ Streaming Platforms

When we walk in after a long day at work and just feel like watching mindless television shows, what are those?

_____   _____

_____   _____

_____   _____

Are you like me and sometimes watch television before going to bed? I was struck by how much my dreams were mimicking any negativity that I subconsciously had picked up on from television shows. When I changed my television diet, I noticed I had less fearful and negative dreams.

SO, LET'S TALK ABOUT INPUT: Habits and Places We Frequent

"I don't like going to the same church anymore."

Triggers that can bring up bad memories or make us feel negative (sad, bad, less-than etc.):

- Being around happily married couples.
- Being around couples we use to spend time with as a couple.
- Certain restaurants we used to go to together.
- Automatically answering the phone when our ex calls.
- Attending the gym we used to attend together.
- Church where many know our story and we have to answer a lot of questions.

What environments come to your mind that bring up negative/fearful/sad thoughts or emotions?

_____   _____

_____   _____

_____   _____

THIS HURTS! CUT IT OUT!

"Learn from yesterday. Don't live in it."
Dr. Tony Evans

What we surround ourselves with affects us. People and places – whether they're actual people in our lives or those on TV or social media – all impact us. If you're anything like me, during the initial stages of the divorce, I was very vulnerable, and I found myself more easily influenced by my environment.

I DON'T WANT TO SHUT PEOPLE OUT OF MY LIFE!

It's not forever, it's just for now. So, what am I suggesting? Cutting out negative people, places and things… for now.

Let's go back to our analogy of being around someone who has strong breath from garlic and onions and ask ourselves, "Does that mean we never go around that friend again?" No, of course not. We might keep a distance for a while, and when we feel ready to re-engage, we do. It's the same with our diet of negativity. We don't go without seeing friends or family members forever, without watching the news forever, or blocking people we love on social media forever. It's not forever, it's just for now. It's just for the initial stages of our **triage and breathe.**

When you stop focusing on the negative voices inside and around you, your path becomes clear. You can hear God's true voice, determine your unique purpose, live free. Who and what you listen to is a choice.

Choose freedom.

p.s. Negativity can include your ex.

SOME REAL EXAMPLES:

"Communicating with my ex sends me spiraling!"

As Lynn tells it:

"When I got on the phone with my ex, I would scream at him and get so mad! I had a hard time sleeping after talking to him. I realized he brought out the worst side of me, and it was actually bad for my self-esteem – not only because of the things he said or did but mainly because I didn't like the version of me that came out over the phone. Once I realized this and shared it with my therapist, he encouraged me to make boundaries for communication with my ex. He suggested I give my ex the options of email or text. I texted my ex to tell him I would not talk to him on the phone anymore.

I realized if I was going to regain my self-esteem and stop losing ground, I had to limit the times that were bringing out the worst in me, and talking with him over the phone was one of them. Now, I only allow our conversations to be via text or email. It didn't work overnight. He still kept trying to call me. I wouldn't answer. I would respond by text saying, "I'm not able to talk by phone. What do you need?"

With text and email, I give myself time to process my response. I sometimes sleep on it before I send it, and I have even deleted messages after typing them. If we need to discuss something over the phone, I ask about the topic and I can plan the conversation. Even seeing his name on my caller ID still makes my heart race."

I loved Barbara's phone trick:

"I kept regretting when I would call or text my ex. It usually happened later at night, after I had a couple of glasses of wine. Then I came up with a solution. If I was drinking, I'd give my phone to a girlfriend. If we were home, I'd put my phone in the fridge. If I was tempted to call/text/post at least holding onto that cold brick phone would wake me up a bit and it gave me a moment to pause before I called/texted/posted something I'd later regret. It worked! The only downside was leaving home without it. I got to work one day and realized I didn't have my phone. I had to laugh. I knew it was waiting for me safely stored in my fridge!"

Reminder: Every single thing that is written can be used in a court of law. Barbara was smart to do this, not only because she didn't say something she'd later regret, but she also didn't text something that could later be used against her in divorce mediation and proceedings.

This step of cutting out the negative is not about thriving, yet. We're talking about survival. It takes longer to heal when we still allow negativity into our lives. This is the time to focus on ourselves. It's been said, "As we think we become," and we all know that what we feed grows. If we feed the negativity, negativity grows. If we feed positivity, positivity grows. To create a new future, it only makes sense that we need to add positive influences and experiences to our lives right now.

TIME FOR THE POSITIVE: Common Friends

Well, what about the friends that you have in common with your ex? That's a tough one. If you're like me, you may need to put a pause on those relationships.

When I did, it helped to have those relationships come back around four and a half years later, but the initial pause really helped me. I'm a new person now. I am not the same weak and exposed person I was when we separated. And years later, many of the friendships are stronger now, because of the pause I took, as I used that time to work on myself.

Here are a few ideas on how to put a pause on these friendships:

- Not accept invitations to be with them for a period of 6 to 12 months (or longer).
- Not follow them on social media temporarily.
- Make holiday plans that do not include them.

TIME FOR THE POSITIVE: Do We Stay on Social Media? If So, Who Do We Continue to Follow?

Here's a quiz for those who want to stay on social media:

Do you follow your ex?	YES NO
Do you follow friends who you used to hang out with as a couple?	YES NO
Do you follow draining/negative/sarcastic people?	YES NO
Do you follow people or pages that remind you of your time together?	YES NO
Do you follow people you feel are on your ex-spouse's "side?"	YES NO

The unfortunate truth is there are people that will take sides. You can temporarily limit exposure to those people in your life.

We will each have different responses to the questions above. Some of us do not engage on social media at all, and others find social media as an effective tool in our business or social lives. We each have unique ways to navigate this age of social media.

I even put on pause friends who were negative about politics or looked at things sarcastically. We don't need to block them forever, but we can "mute" them for a period of time. Initially, I was concerned they would notice and it could hurt their feelings. Thankfully, most of the time on social media, they don't even know that you've blocked or muted them. The result of limiting the negative input is that you'll notice the feed to your brain becomes more and more positive.

I stayed on social media throughout and at a certain point, I answered NO to all the questions above. It wasn't all at once, and it wasn't always forever. Again, it's an individual decision, but I found the above to be helpful questions to ask as I was trying to figure out my anger, fear, and depression triggers. By answering "NO" to all of the above questions, I was eliminating many of my negative triggers.

TIME FOR THE POSITIVE: Positive Social Media, Television and Radio

This helped me so much. You can probably already tell who I have in my social media feed based on people I quote: Dr. Caroline Leaf, Christine Cain, Dr. Henry Cloud, John Maxwell, Michael Hyatt, Steven Covey, Andy Stanley and his dad, Dr. Charles Stanley.

Here are some ideas to build the positive influences into your life:

- Add good influences on radio and social media feeds of your favorite inspirational speaker.
- Add 10 groups on each social media platform to follow. Just type in the words "positive," "inspirational"

or "happy" and you'll have a selection of choices to suit your taste.
- I also went to the search bar and typed in the hashtags #positivequotes, #positivememes, and #inspirationalquotes. I scrolled through and started following people or organizations who were posting consistent positive and inspirational content.
- Heard a good TED Talk? Search for their name in your social media and follow them.
- Add your church to your feed if it's not a negative place for you right now. If your church has separate accounts for other ministries within the church you can add those (i.e., kid's ministry, women's ministries, outreach ministries, etc.)
- If your church is on your list of negative places right now, follow a different church in your area or anywhere around the nation.
- On some social platforms you can see who other people follow. Follow the first couple they follow.
- What are a few organizations making an impact in the area you care about (the environment, homeless, disaster relief, animal rescue, etc.)? Follow them! Ideas: Homeless – Habitat for Humanity; Disaster Relief – Samaritan's Purse, etc.
- Add other uplifting ministries who you've heard on radio or television.
Ideas: "Better Together" – Women's Encouragement, Lisa Harper – Hilarious, down to earth Bible Teacher, etc.

By adding the positive, we're diluting the negative.

HOW TO DIVORCE WELL

I bought a new car that came with free satellite radio. I was excited about it. I took advantage of it by listening to a pastor who was someone I normally wouldn't listen to. He was all about self-help and feeling better. During the darkest days, inspirational Christian radio stations were all I listened to.

Even if I wasn't "listening" I was subconsciously feeding my mind with positive messages. It helped drown out the barrage of negativity that would flood my mind in silence. I listened until my free membership ran out. Then, I didn't listen to that particular pastor anymore. Listening to him served its purpose for a time, and it helped me through some very dark days.

When it comes to positive voices on the radio and in social media, who comes to mind?

_____

_____

_____

TIME FOR THE POSITIVE: Choose Battery Charging, Not Battery Draining Friends

My mom used to say about her friendships, "There are battery chargers and battery drainers in life." Right now is the time to eliminate negative, battery draining friends.

Battery drainers are people who often default to negativity and point out others' shortcomings (or their own flaws). Often, battery drainers mask their cynicism by using humor or sarcasm. They may consistently call attention to inadequacies with their responses, comments, or stares. Negative people

THIS HURTS! CUT IT OUT!

will view circumstances from a cynical perspective, assuming the worst in a situation. When walking away from being around a battery drainer, there is often a feeling that someone was put down or made to feel inferior.

Who comes to mind?

_____

_____

_____

"Won't my life feel even emptier?"

What if you think you're lonely enough already and by eliminating more people from your life it will end up even emptier? You might be surprised. Even without replacing that person, you end up further in the positive, because you're no longer being drained.

> *"Make no friendship with a man given to anger, nor go with a wrathful man."*
> (Proverbs 22:24 ESV)

Instead...

> *"...whatever is true, whatever is noble, whatever is right, whatever is pure, whatever is lovely, whatever is admirable – if anything is excellent or praiseworthy – think about such things."*
> (Philippians 4:8 NIV)

We are going to continually feel more and more empty if we choose to surround ourselves with negativity, sarcasm, and anger. If we don't shut out those influences, we shouldn't be surprised if we are depressed, angry, and resentful. We need to be careful.

What if you're talking about lifelong friends or family? Just remember, this isn't forever. We have a limited amount of energy right now. We need to guard it!

TIME FOR THE POSITIVE: Turn Fears into Prayers
"What do I do with the racing thoughts and fears that constantly come to mind?" The key right now is to change negative thoughts into positive and productive thoughts. As I mentioned before, I have a prayer card system. Whenever I'm nervous, anxious, or scared, I always write my fear on a little index card. I thoroughly describe whatever is making me nervous, anxious, angry, or scared at that moment.

PRAYER CARD PROCESS – For instance, if you're woken in the middle of the night.
1. In a journal or on notecards, write down the fear. "I'm scared about how I'm going to pay the bills."
2. Put it next to your bed and try to get back to sleep.
3. In the morning, cross out "I'm scared about," and replace it with, "God solve"
"God solve how I'm going to pay the bills."
4. Put that in the area you'll see it regularly.
5. Just say it out loud or quietly to yourself.

I read the cards every morning and it turns my fears, anxieties, and anger into prayer requests for God to handle. The simple act of writing down my fear and putting it on an index card did a few things:

THIS HURTS! CUT IT OUT!

1. It helped stop me from obsessing about it. God has it.
2. It turned it from a fear to faith that somehow there would be a resolution.
3. It helped me remember it in prayer every day.

Was I THAT Unstable and Fragile?

Yup. I went back through my prayer cards, and after a few months, I saw how small my requests were. I know it was a reflection of how low my self-esteem and expectations had fallen. My initial prayer cards said I wanted a job. Now I want a new career. So, I changed my prayer card and crossed out the word job and wrote career instead.

This was one of mine:

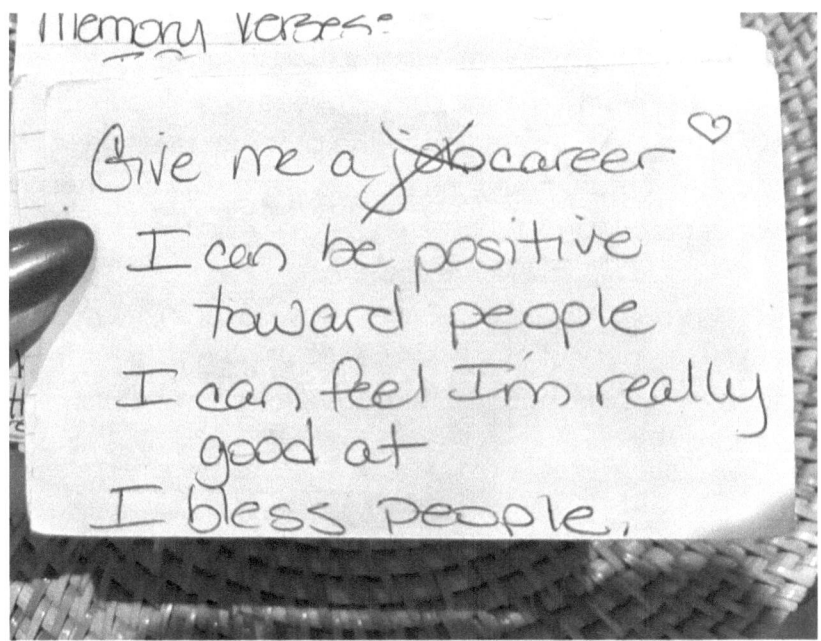

HOW TO DIVORCE WELL

It changed the prayer. I was asking from such a limiting way of thinking, and it changed to a more realistic way of thinking. I started praying to ask God to help me build a future, a bigger picture, a purpose-driven career. This was a completely different way of looking at the same problem.

> *"This day I call heaven and earth as witnesses against you that I have set before you life and death, blessing and curses. Now choose life, so that you and your children may live and that you may love the Lord your God, listen to His voice and hold fast to Him."*
> (Deuteronomy 30:19-20)

TIME FOR THE POSITIVE: Give to Others

"I'm feeling so depressed and can't seem to get away from my feelings of hopelessness."

When I felt discouraged, I went out and encouraged people. When I felt rejected, I went out and tried to make others feel welcome – whether in my place of business, the local coffee shop, in the produce section at the grocery store, or with a homeless woman. If anyone looked like they were feeling down or discouraged, I tried to share a smile.[4]

Notice the common thread, "I went out..." Even in my sweats, I needed to get out of the house. Fresh air and a change of scenery can make a tremendous difference in our entire demeanor.

---

[4] *This is not to take the place of help for clinical depression. Please seek proper medical help if you think you are dealing with clinical or situational depression.*

THIS HURTS! CUT IT OUT!

TIME FOR THE POSITIVE: Acts of Kindness Journal

"I catch myself feeling like such a failure!"

My girlfriend was wise enough to give me an "Acts of Kindness" journal. She said I needed to stop and recognize when I was doing kind things for others. That was COMPLETELY against the way I was raised. I believed we weren't supposed to celebrate or acknowledge ourselves when we did kind things. I had learned we do them in private, "for our Father above to see."

Well, that was incorrect thinking. After all, I wasn't telling others, I was telling myself. My girlfriend was simply giving me a tool to help remind myself that I was doing acts of kindness. I realized recognizing those moments made me not feel like such a failure, or so bad about my day. In fact, it often made me more intentional about doing even more acts of kindness. It became a self-perpetuating loop of continuing kindness. Doing acts of kindness improves our self-esteem.

What are three acts of kindness you've done recently?   EXAMPLES
1. _____ (held the door for someone)
2. _____ (smiled at someone)
3. _____ (told your kids "I love you")

Try writing them down nightly. You might be surprised at the impact it will have on your self-esteem.

IDEAS:
Tip your server.
Return your shopping cart.
Pick up a piece of trash.
Hold the door for the person behind you. Let someone into your lane. Pay for the coffee.
Small acts can have a ripple effect. That's how we change the world.

TIME FOR THE POSITIVE: Remember the Hard Things You've Done and be Proud!

If you're anything like me, instead of praising myself for all the hard things I've done, instead of keeping track of everything I'm proud of, I ruminate on all I haven't gotten done yet. I naturally focus on projects left undone, and what I could do better. Can you relate?

> Tip your server.
> Return your shopping cart.
> Pick up a piece of trash.
> Hold the door for the person behind you.
> Let someone into your lane.
> Small acts can have a ripple effect. That's how we change the world.
> #HowToDivorceWell

Do you feel you have so much to do and you're not getting enough done? I stayed focused on all that hadn't been completed on my to-do lists. That made me feel discouraged and defeated. I started making a list of the hard things I was doing, and the difficult things I had accomplished, starting from the time of our separation. I had to remember how hard certain things were.

THIS HURTS! CUT IT OUT!

There were things I didn't imagine I could do, and I did it!

Name three difficult things you've done since the start of your divorce/separation:

1. _____

2. _____

3. _____

BRAVO! I wrote my three things down and kept them in an area where I was sure to read them at least once a day. Remembering that I had done hard things in the past gave me more confidence and courage to do hard things in the future.

You'll likely find yourself adding to your list.

TIME FOR THE POSITIVE: Communication with Our Ex

"When my ex calls, I go spiraling!"

Yep – pretty common. We still need to communicate with our ex. We can't just avoid them, especially when we're in the middle of divorce and we have children together. The fix is not eliminating communication. We can only fix what is within our control. The time, way, and frequency of our communication with our ex *are* within our control.

HOW TO DIVORCE WELL

Texting Better

What do we want to say? "Stupid idiot, Just like always, you've forgotten to pay the electric bill. Thanks a lot for putting all this stress on me again, you jerk. You wonder why I want a divorce!?" Yup. We can still feel that we just don't have to type that.

I prefer the "sandwich approach" text: "Good morning. I need you to pay your portion of the bill. Thanks for taking time to handle this."

GOOD (I use a common nicety): Good morning.

REQUEST (the reason why we're contacting them): I need you to pay your portion of the bill.

GOOD (affirming their intent or response): Thanks for taking time to handle this.

Does that feel weird? Yes, but beginning the communication with a common nicety opens up a calm dialogue and makes room for a more positive response.

Example of a difficult topic I need to mention to my ex:

_____

What's an example of a conversation or text you might have with your ex:

GOOD (use a common nicety):

_____

THIS HURTS! CUT IT OUT!

REQUEST (the reason why you're contacting them):

_____

GOOD (affirming their intent or response):

_____

Is it easy? No. Is it worth it? Yes. We don't want to stay where we currently are. Our goal is to get to the other side of the pain, anger, and frustration of our divorce. We want to put the divorce behind us and grow into a better version of ourselves for the next chapter of our lives.

So, agreeing to cut out the negative communication and replace it with good is a low effort, big pay-off proposition.

It's very simple yet can be incredibly difficult. Our relationships are complex. Let's recapture some groundwork together below:

DID YOU (LIKE ME) TRY SOME COUNTERFEIT COMFORTS?

When I was going through the worst of the divorce, I reached for anything to hold back the feelings of impending doom. I wanted ANYTHING to mask or numb those floodgates of pain and discouragement... even if only temporarily. I wanted anything just to get through TODAY.

HOW TO DIVORCE WELL

Dan's 30-pound divorce:

"My divorce didn't just cost me a fortune financially, it cost me my health. I started stress eating. I didn't realize it, because for the first time in 10 years, I was having to cook for myself. Instead of cooking, I ate out a lot. Any food I would cook myself was pre-made and often unhealthy. From what I know now, it's harder to lose weight when we're stressed. Well, my new diet coupled with the stress of the divorce added up to a 30-pound problem. Once I was ready to date, I didn't blame women for not giving me a second look. *I* didn't even like the way I looked. At my annual physical, (which I missed two years in a row), my doctor informed me I not only needed to lose a few pounds, but my blood pressure was too high, and I was starting to deal with high cholesterol. I'm still struggling to get back in shape."

Are you like so many of us? Have you started over-shopping, over-eating, over-spending, focusing on other people's lives (including our ex), over-drinking, or over-*anything* that can hurt us in the future?

A friend and colleague, Robia Scott, has written a book by just that name: "Counterfeit Comforts." In her book, she deals with the core issues that cause us to run to something that doesn't serve us, like over-drinking, over-eating, etc. What helped me snap out of it was when I put on my metaphorical "future glasses." What did I need in the future? I couldn't afford to get stuck in the past. I knew my energy and time were limited resources, and I needed 100% of myself running on all cylinders to focus my time to create a positive future, not one with even more liabilities.

THIS HURTS! CUT IT OUT!

Well, there's good news and bad news.

If we're using unhealthy coping mechanisms to get ourselves through this time of our lives, we're not alone. Whether it's shopping, working, drinking, eating, sex, spending – there are others of us out there that can relate to your coping mechanism. We sometimes look for anything to take away or dull the pain of loneliness and the fear of the days ahead. These coping mechanisms work for us until they don't. The bad news? I couldn't find a single person I interviewed who didn't overdo it in one or more of these areas for at least a short time when going through their divorce. But there's hope.

How are you doing with excesses?

Over-eating? Over-drinking? Over-spending? Are you doing anything you'll pay for later? If you need to go to a support group such as EDA (Eating Disorders Anonymous), Alcoholics Anonymous (AA), or Gambler's Anonymous, it's nothing to be ashamed about. It doesn't mean you're addicted. It means you don't want to go down that road. If you have a desire to stop overdoing any of these things, the support groups are designed to give us tools. It's a way to help ourselves NOW. This is survival mode, we're not thriving yet. This can be a step to stop us from going down a path that creates further negative repercussions for ourselves.

We've probably all heard of Alcoholics Anonymous (AA), and likely you've heard there are specialty support groups like Cocaine Anonymous, Meth, or Nicotine, but did you know there's also Compulsive Shopping Disorder Anonymous?

HOW TO DIVORCE WELL

Yep, according to Healthline Magazine[5], nearly 18 million Americans are considered to have this addiction. Who knew? Circle ones that you think could be helpful for you:

- ACA – Adult Children of Alcoholics for those who were raised in alcoholic and other dysfunctional families
- Al-Anon/Alateen, for friends and families of alcoholics, associated with AA
- CLA – Clutterers Anonymous
- Co-Anon, for friends and family of cocaine addicts, associated with Cocaine Anonymous
- CoDA – Co-Dependents Anonymous, for people working to end patterns of dysfunctional relationships and develop functional and healthy relationships
- COSA – a friends and family group associated with Sex Addicts Anonymous
- COSLAA – CoSex and Love Addicts Anonymous, for friends and family of people with a sex or love addiction, associated with SLAA
- DA – Debtors Anonymous
- EA – Emotions Anonymous, for recovery from mental and emotional illness
- FA – Families Anonymous, for relatives and friends of addicts
- FA – Food Addicts in Recovery Anonymous
- FAA – Food Addicts Anonymous
- GA – Gamblers Anonymous
- Gam-Anon/Gam-A-Teen, for friends and family members of problem gamblers
- N/A – Neurotics Anonymous, for recovery from mental and emotional illness

---

[5] https://www.healthline.com/health/addiction/shopping

THIS HURTS! CUT IT OUT!

- Nar-Anon, for friends and family members of addicts
- OA – Overeaters Anonymous
- PA – Pills Anonymous, for recovery from prescription pill addiction
- RA – Racists Anonymous
- SA – Sexaholics Anonymous
- SAA – Sex Addicts Anonymous
- SCA – Sexual Compulsives Anonymous
- SIA – Survivors of Incest Anonymous
- SLAA – Sex and Love Addicts Anonymous
- SRA – Sexual Recovery Anonymous
- UA – Underearners Anonymous
- WA – Workaholics Anonymous

Any number of these could be helpful to just visit. Does that mean we're an addict? No, not necessarily. We can attend and say we're an "observer" (as I have done), and you can find encouragement and hope to release the tendencies to over-*anything*.

Group meeting information can be found with a simple internet search. Don't have time to drive to a meeting? Is the closest one too far away? There are many meetings online now. You can listen in on your lunch break or while driving.

If you know you have a problem, please know you can seek one-on-one treatment, 24-hour care, or even outpatient programs where insurance is often accepted. Know if you're reading this and something has stirred in you, I'm praying for you. You deserve help, freedom, and encouragement.

We don't always have control over what is happening. By intentionally and actively eliminating the negativity and

HOW TO DIVORCE WELL

adding positivity into our lives, it doesn't change what's happening, but it changes our environment and that can make all the difference.

CHAPTER 6

PAUSE! STOP HERE.

You're doing great! We're almost ready to move on and design your new life to thrive after divorce. Are you ready? Let's ask ourselves some questions first. How are you doing in the four areas we've already discussed?

> TRIAGE/ BREATHE AND STABILIZE: "…I've got my basic needs covered but I'm not taking time for self-care yet…"
>
> or
>
> FORGIVENESS: "…Okay. Okay. I've said, 'I forgive you. I'm ready to move on…"
>
> or
>
> 3-AT-3: "…Yeah. Yeah. I've got a couple of people I can call when I need to."
>
> or
>
> CUT OUT THE NEGATIVE: "…I'm still working on cutting all the negative people, places and things out of my life. You can't expect me to do this overnight!"

HOW TO DIVORCE WELL

Yes. Exactly. What it takes to do the work in the first five chapters outlined in this book does not happen overnight. **This is where many of us who are newly divorced people go wrong.** We unwillingly, unknowingly, and unintentionally create chaos and FUTURE ADDITIONAL PROBLEMS by making decisions to move on before we're fully healed and have clarity of mind and necessary tools in our tool belts. In fact, many people move on to make big decisions they later regret. We don't need to follow in their footsteps. Let's learn from their mistakes.

If you're anything like me, I wanted to heal quickly. I wanted to get on with my life. Sound familiar? Yeah, me too. Sorry to be the bearer of bad news, but it doesn't quite work that way. But let's go with it for a minute. Let's say we did heal quickly and were ready to start our new lives. To see if we're ready, let's give ourselves a score sheet right now on all four of the concepts in the previous chapters:

> We unwillingly, unknowingly, and unintentionally create chaos and FUTURE ADDITIONAL PROBLEMS by making decisions to move on before we're fully healed and have clarity of mind
> #HowToDivorceWell

* Note: The numerical grading scales are different for each category. Consider the first number the lowest, and the last number the highest. For instance:

1   5   10   15   20   25

In the above example, 1 would be the lowest on the scale, and 25 would be the greatest. Circle your answers.

PAUSE! STOP HERE.

TRIAGE/PRIORITIZE AND BREATHE/STABILIZE

	Disagree					Agree
I've identified what stage I'm currently in	0	2	4	6	8	10

(Wake-up/Shock) (Triage) (Breathe/Stabilize) (Market Yourself) (Launch 2.0 You!)

I wrote out and read aloud affirmations	0	2	4	6	8	10
I'm getting enough sleep	0	2	4	6	8	10
I attend counseling/divorce care support	0	2	4	6	8	10
I've legally protected myself	0	2	4	6	8	10
I've financially protected myself	0	2	4	6	8	10
I make enough to cover expenses	0	2	4	6	8	10
I've created boundaries with my ex	0	2	4	6	8	10
I've communicated boundaries	0	2	4	6	8	10
I'm waiting to date	0	2	4	6	8	10

My Total TRIAGE/BREATHE Assessment _____

FORGIVENESS

FORGIVENESS Assessment	Disagree				Agree
I forgive my ex in my mind	0	5	10	15	20
When bad memories come, I quickly forgive	0	5	10	15	20
I have no desire for retribution	0	5	10	15	20
I have forgiven myself	0	5	10	15	20
I practice ongoing forgiveness of myself	0	5	10	15	20

My Total FORGIVENESS Assessment _____

3-at-3

3-at-3 Assessment	Disagree				Agree
I have three people who I connect with regularly	0	10	20	30	40	50
I've filled in names in all my concentric circles	0	10	20	30	40	50

My Total 3-at-3 Assessment _____

PAUSE! STOP HERE.

CUT OUT THE NEGATIVE

Cut Out the Negative Assessment Disagree   Agree

I've cut out negative input in these areas:

Social Media feed(s)	0	5	10	15	20	25
Television	0	5	10	15	20	25
People I choose to be around	0	5	10	15	20	25
Old hangouts which bring up memories that trigger shame, anger, guilt, sadness, etc.	0	5	10	15	20	25

My Total Cut Out the Negative Assessment _____

Fill in the percentage according to your self-assessment above. For example:

Assessment Total was 90,
I would fill in the circle like this:

If my FORGIVENESS
Assessment Total was 70,
I would fill in the circle like this:

HOW TO DIVORCE WELL

Now it's your turn!

Your circles:

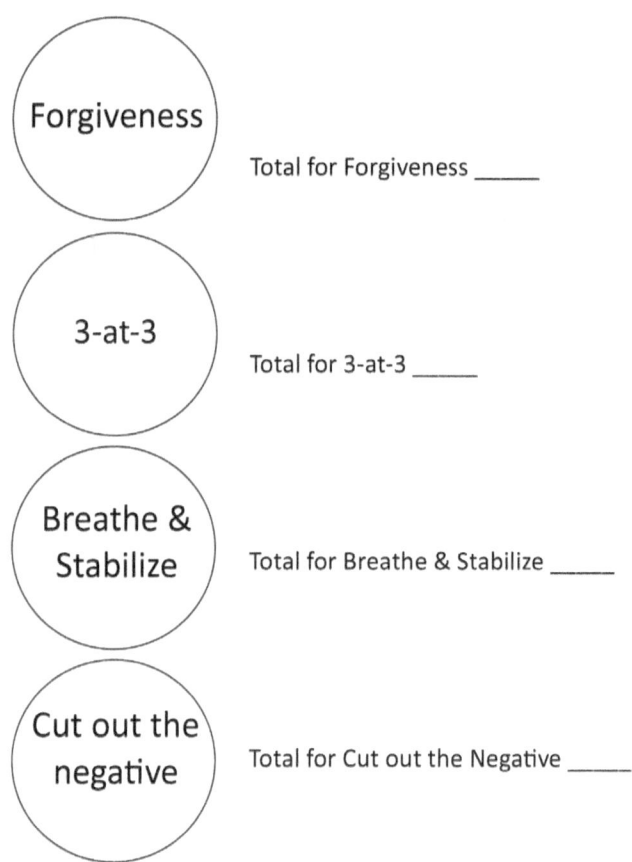

Now, let's flip the page and fill out each of the corresponding circles.

PAUSE! STOP HERE.

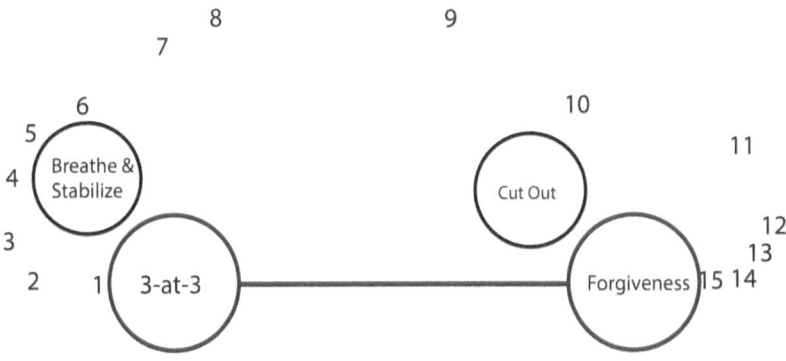

Now, connect the dots, 1 through 15. See the car and its wheels? That's your current car and how full its wheels are to start moving forward. Are you ready to go forward? Although no one can expect to be 100% great at all these areas, my estimation is that we can still drive forward (albeit slowly and very cautiously) with our tires about 80% full. How are you doing? Ready to go forward? Great. Skip to Chapter 7. Bye… see you there!

Are you like me and many others and need to revisit or fill up a tire or two? Well, like you, for the first couple of years, I was not quite at 80% in all tires. I needed air in a few. I had to ask myself, "Why does anger keep popping up? Is it because I can't fully forgive yet?" Or maybe you haven't had the chance to get a hold of three people. After all, that was only two chapters ago! Or maybe you don't have three people you can trust. Cutting out people, places and things takes time.

You may be thinking, "You don't get it. My situation is so much harder and more complex than you are explaining." I understand. It was very hard for me at the beginning as well. The key is to be aware of where we need to focus to shore up our weakest areas so we can move forward with strength, confidence, and stability.

Let's break it down and do it together.

First let's turn back to Chapter 4 and look at our second circle in our Concentric Circle. Let's look at the circle just outside of our 3-at-3. These are the professionals in our lives who we can count on for support as they know the relative details of our divorce situation. How much support do you feel you have in the following areas?

- Family – I feel _____% known by the supportive people in my immediate family. I have reached out.
- Doctor – I feel _____% checked in with my primary physician. They know about my divorce.
- Minister – I feel _____% known by a spiritual leader/confidant in my place of worship.
- Attorney – I feel my legal needs are _____% covered.
- Divorce Coach – If I need additional help beyond this book, I feel _____% confident I can benefit from Divorce Well Support Group, 1-on-1 Divorce Coaching, or a How to Divorce Well Course.
- Therapist / Counselor – If I need it, I am _____% confident I have a therapist to support me.
- Accountant / Financial Advisor – If I need it, I am _____% confident I have an accountant and/or financial advisor to support me.

We can do this! We can't thrive in life without having a solid foundation. And yeah, this is where I stalled. I needed to slow down here because my legal and financial underpinnings and infrastructure needed to be shored up.

PAUSE! STOP HERE.

NOW IS THE TIME TO REACH OUT

Who will you be reaching out to this week for support?

I'll reach out to _____
for a recommendation/referral in _____

I'll reach out to _____
for a recommendation/referral in _____

I'll reach out to _____
for a recommendation/referral in _____

"HOW DO I MOVE FORWARD WITH STRENGTH, CONFIDENCE, AND STABILITY?"

Let's keep going together and see how we can further shore up those areas. First of all, I get it. You're not alone. If you're frustrated, overwhelmed, or even scared, please don't feel like you've been left behind in the back of the class. It's not as if you're being told you're not allowed to be promoted to the next grade and graduate with your classmates. It's not that way.

> The foundation we've been talking about is critical for us to move forward and build a healthy new chapter of our lives where we thrive after divorce.
> #HowToDivorceWell

The truth is healing takes time.

HOW TO DIVORCE WELL

The foundation we've been talking about is critical for us to move forward and build a healthy new chapter of our lives where we thrive after divorce.

We all know people who have gotten divorced quickly, moved to get as far away from their ex as possible, or changed careers, or dated immediately afterwards, or made big financial decisions. Hasty decisions made without sound healing often lead to decisions we later regret.

If we take the time to build a healthy healing foundation, big winds of discouragement and the everyday difficulties of life are not as likely to knock us out. In my experience and many others, the right home, the right job, and the right relationship will all be waiting for you. If we heal well, we will be a better version of ourselves to go into the next season. Think of it as (Your Name Here) version 2.0.

Are there any of these four categories where you're needing help? You and I can break them down into smaller pieces and work on them together. If you think additional tools would help, I encourage you to invest in the accompanying course you'll see available at the end of this book.

If you feel you'd benefit from one-on-one personalized time, let's set up a strategy session to see if it would work to walk through this with you. You can always contact your therapist, pastor, etc. However, after you navigate these initial waters and make an honest assessment of where you stand, I encourage you to take your time. Give yourself time to hone in on each area thoroughly.

PAUSE! STOP HERE.

You're not being graded. This is not a race. I was not able to have a thriving life without having a firm foundation in these four areas first. And keep our organization in your back pocket – We are a call, email, or a strategy session away. We can do it together.

Check out the positive people that you've identified in chapters one through four. Look into their books, their podcasts, etc. Whether you listen to Caroline Leaf's podcasts, start following inspirational and positive accounts on social media, have weekly therapy sessions, join one of my How to Divorce Well Courses, the How to Divorce Well group on Facebook, email our organization for a strategy session, or one-on-one coaching, I applaud you for taking the time to heal well. You are giving yourself the best opportunity to develop a healthy new life.

Let's see how we can work together to keep building the best version of YOU! But what if…

CHAPTER 7

I DON'T LIKE THE ME I SEE

"Everything gets harder if you start going on and on about how hard it is."
— MD Wilson

"I don't have anything to be grateful for right now. My life is a mess."

"I'm having a hard time moving forward. My ex caused me way too much pain and I'm still dealing with all of the ramifications of their horrible behavior."

"I'm struggling with feeling defeated and depressed."

"I feel like when I take one step forward, I get knocked three steps back."

"If you're going to ask me to do a gratitude list, I'm NOT in the mood!"

HOW TO DIVORCE WELL

In the initial months of my divorce, I wasn't sleeping or making time for regular doctor appointments. My self-esteem was in the tank, and as for my mental strength, I couldn't think my way out of a paper bag. If you're feeling any of these things or relate to the quotes above, you're not alone. Go grab a journal and fill in your answers on the column to the right. I've given examples from some of our contributors.

Let's focus on a few areas that could help us with…

Improved physical health	_____ *(e.g.) …lose the weight I'm putting on*
Improved psychological health	_____ *(e.g.) …think more clearly for work*
Sleeping better	_____ *(e.g.) …think more clearly for work*
Improved self-esteem	_____ *(e.g.) …minimize the negative talk in my head*
Improved mental strength	_____ *(e.g.) …think clearer to make decisions*
Enhanced empathy	_____ *(e.g.) …be sensitive to people around me and*
Reduced aggressive behaviors	_____ *(e.g) …lash out less at my ex (have less regrets)*
Opening doors to relationships	_____ *(e.g.) …get more support and possibly meet someone new one day*

I DON'T LIKE THE ME I SEE

Here's a hint at where we start

Scientific research leads us to understand that gratitude helps us sleep better, improve both our physical and psychological health, open doors to more relationships, enhance our empathy, reduce aggressive behaviors, improve our self-esteem, and improve our overall mental strength.
– Adapted from Amy Morin, PsyD
"13 Things Mentally Strong People Don't Do"

Why are we doing this exercise? Let's look at where we are. We've discussed the stages of **shock/wake-up**, you've **triaged/prioritized** and are starting to **breathe/stabilize**. As you've gotten your **3-at-3** in place, **cut out the negative** input that's in your control, now it's time to start using tools to help you become **marketable** and design the **2.0 version** of your new life.

(Wake-up/Shock) (Triage) (Breathe/Stabilize) (**MARKET YOURSELF**) (Launch 2.0 You!)

HOW CAN WE START TO MARKET OURSELVES FOR OUR NEXT CHAPTER?

Great question. If we're down in the dumps, we first need to find some tools to get out of the dumps and gratitude is a key to get us started!

> *"In broader terms, gratitude increases happiness and positive mood, gives us more satisfaction with life, makes us less materialistic, less likely to experience burnout, experience less fatigue, have lower levels of cellular inflammation, develop greater resiliency, and encourages the development of patience, humility, and wisdom."*
> – Excerpts from Emmons and Mishra (2011)
> "Why Gratitude Enhances Well-Being: What We Know, What We Need to Know."

If it's true, "God inhabits the praises of his people," what does that mean? I like the way Succeed in Life Church puts it in this adapted explanation of this concept:

> Psalm 22 says that God inhabits the praises of Israel, and that means if we lived in a constant state of praising God, it would cause Him to dwell in us. That's His promise. Wherever God's presence is, His light and life are there as well. True praise isn't singing Christian music 24 hours a day or shouting hallelujah like a religious fanatic. Praise is not done for others to see, or to gratify our flesh. It's a personal expression of faith in God that can be seen in the attitudes we choose, what we say and do, and by directing our minds to constantly return to Him for nourishment throughout

the day... every day. Choosing to show kindness to someone as a means of honoring God, even when our kindness is unlikely to be returned, is an act of praise.

Rejecting the emotional pull of anger or pride and choosing thankfulness to God instead is an act of praise as well. Determining that His promises will come true to such a degree that we act as if they've already been granted, is another act of praise. Praise is much more than a church ritual. It's a way of living out our faith."

Could you use a little help from God right now?

Maybe it sounds odd and counter intuitive, but if you're in a bad place, find something to thank God for. If you're in pain and anxious, start thinking of things to thank God for. He's there, in that exact moment. He inhabits the praises of his people. Crazy, right? Try it. It works!

As one of my favorite authors and speakers, neuroscientist Dr. Caroline Leaf says,

"... [when we] look beyond what we are going through and remember how much we have to be thankful for... and choose to develop a gratitude mindset... when times are tough, we can increase our longevity, our ability to use our imagination, our overall health and our ability to **problem-solve**! An 'attitude of gratitude' actually leads to the feeling that life is worth living, which brings mental health benefits in a positive feedback loop, strengthening the mind and improving our resilience, which, in turn, **helps us bounce back more quickly when life gets tough**."

HOW TO DIVORCE WELL

In her article "How to Build Mental Toughness" (November 14, 2018), Dr. Leaf goes on to explain, "It is so important to remember that our thoughts can improve our peace, health, vision, toughness, strength, and much more. Mental toughness overflows into every area of our lives and gives us the ability to persevere and pursue our dreams."

Are you struggling with your mindset?

If you are like me and happen to struggle with thoughts of feeling defeated and depressed during this time, I highly recommend Dr. Leaf's online 21 Day Brain Detox Challenge. She is a Christian neuropsychologist (brain doctor) who gives tangible steps to help us rewire our thinking.

How do you become grateful? I made a very specific appointment with myself every morning to write down at least three things I was grateful for. Once I started it, some days my list became very, very long. Then there were days I had only three things I could be grateful for:

1. I woke up.
2. I didn't hurt myself.
3. I didn't hurt anyone else.

That actually was my list for more days than I care to admit. If you're feeling the same, it's okay. It's a process. We can't expect to be bubbling over with gratitude when we're going through one of the hardest seasons of our lives. It doesn't happen overnight. I had to find one small thing each morning that I was grateful for.

I DON'T LIKE THE ME I SEE

Is it easy to do? No. Is it a contrary action? Yes. Why do it if I don't feel like it? It works.

FIVE WAYS TO FEEL BETTER FAST

The old saying goes, "How do I build my self-esteem? By doing esteem-able acts!"

1. Give

We can bring others anything that could help them that you have right now. What you DO have to give right now. Encouragement? Time? Money? Emotional Strength? Resources? Connections? In my experience, it's rare to have abundance in all areas at the same time. When we have money, maybe we don't have emotional strength. When we have emotional reserves and the ability to encourage, maybe we don't have a lot of financial reserves. Think of people who could benefit from what you have to give.

Circle areas of strength for you right now:

MONEY	EMOTIONAL STRENGTH
TIME	RESOURCES
ENCOURAGEMENT	CONNECTIONS

2. Send Notes

I made a very intentional decision to write thank you notes. I would set aside time to write notes to people who did things for me or my kids along the way. Handwritten is best because the 'pen to paper' seems to help focus on the acts of kindness of others, but if you're short on time, an email or text is better than nothing. It got me outside of myself, and it got me into a gratitude mindset. Name three people who did something nice or gave you a gift in the last month.

1. _____

2. _____

3. _____

Now take a quick pause and why not send one of them a quick, 3 sentence handwritten note? How about a text to tell them how grateful you are for them? Note how you feel after you've sent it. Giving to others helps YOU.

3. Give Encouragement

What if you're having a bad day and feeling depressed and insecure? I made sure I kept a list of people who were in dire need of encouragement themselves. I kept it with me in my wallet, not only as a reminder to pray for them, but to send an encouraging text or call when I had a minute. You can be an inspiration and encouragement to someone else who is suffering or having a bad day. It's a great way to get out of ourselves and raise our own self-esteem. Name three people in need of encouragement right now:

1. _____

2. _____

3. _____

If I found myself having a really bad day or having a pity party, I would go help someone else or call someone else who was going through something difficult. I got out of myself and was able to help another in need.

4. Volunteer

Not prepared to deal with people you know right now? Go help strangers! If you're having a bad day, feeling depressed or insecure, maybe it's a good day to sign up to volunteer at a local charity or church. Just the action of taking the initiative to start volunteering is a positive, esteemable act.

"What if I don't WANT to give right now? What if I'm 'gived out'!?!"

Remember, this isn't about what you're doing for *others*, it's our prescription for healing *yourself*. This isn't about what **you feel** like doing. This is what **you've committed** to doing to heal yourself and get to your next chapter. Do we have selfish motives when we're giving to others? Maybe. That's okay. As Nike says, "Just Do It." It works.

"I'll do it when I feel better," didn't work for me.
"I'll do it until I feel better," did.

Just Do It!

Stop reading right now and text someone who did something nice for you this past week. Here are some ideas to get you started:

HOW TO DIVORCE WELL

"Hey, I was just thinking about you, and I wanted to let you know how much I appreciated…

- our talk last week. I needed to process some things, and it really helped."
- our lunch together. Thanks for taking the time. It really meant a lot."
- picking up the kids when I was busy. You're a great friend."

Okay, done. You back? How did that feel?

Do It Daily

Take 10 minutes a day for thank you texts, calls, or thank you notes. Set aside a specific time each day and put a reminder in your phone. If there has been nothing today, think back to a year ago, think back five years ago to when someone did something and reach out to them and say, "Hey, you came to mind today and I just wanted you to know how grateful I am for…" You'll be surprised how people will come out of the woodwork when they feel like you are grateful for them. Reach out. It comes back. Enjoy.

Ever seen the BEFORE and AFTER photos of divorce?

Here's a shallow thought: I find it fascinating to look at photos of couples who have divorced and what each of them looks like a few years later. As I've gotten to know more people who have gone through the painful experience of a divorce, I've found that the way someone looks and gets their life together does not directly correlate to which party was most damaged or "at fault." The person who looks like they're healthy, alive, and thriving can still have financial difficulties or a less than perfect living condition, but they have something in them that shines through – hope.

You can almost see it in time how people age more quickly when they hold on to negativity. People who hold on to resentful and angry thoughts after divorce, look like it. People who move on and focus on gratitude and hope, look like it.

In your mind, what would you like your life to look like in two years? Write out some ideas:

_____

_____

_____

What if I'm still angry and resentful, though?

"What if the divorce is all their fault and I'm not feeling grateful for anything because of all the wreckage they've caused?" Remember this isn't about them. This is about YOU. YOU are the one we're trying to heal. In that case, they simply don't matter. You can try finding at least three things you can be grateful for every morning and every night that have nothing to do with your ex. Make it a ritual. It's a lifestyle. I have gotten to the point that I crave my morning gratitude list. You'll get there. In my experience, when I don't want to forgive and when I don't want to be grateful is when I need to the most.

LET'S PUT IT TO WORK!

**Join me in these few simple commitments I still do daily.
Gratitude Lists**

Step 1 – Week 1
Start with just three items every morning for a week. Just three.

Remember, I admitted on some of the darkest days, my list looked like this:

1. I woke up
2. I stayed alive
3. I helped others stay alive

If you don't feel you have anything to be grateful for, borrow my list until you develop your own. You can also search deeper (i.e. I have eyes to see, ears to hear, legs to walk, etc.).

"Enjoy what you have rather than desiring what you don't have. Just dreaming about nice things is meaningless — like chasing the wind." Ecclesiastes 6:9 NLT

Step 2 – Week 2
Write above the list "Thank you God that… "

1. I woke up
2. I stayed alive
3. I helped others stay alive

(or fill in the blanks).

Step 3 – Week 3
1. Give yourself permission to continue adding to the list
2. Start a gratitude or an acts of kindness list at night before bed.

If you're having a tough time sleeping or having nightmares (I sure was having the CRAZIEST nightmares), a gratitude list before bed really helps. You'll be grateful that you made the change and you'll sleep better.

It won't take long before you'll be thinking clearer. Now that we're getting in a better "head space," many of us feel bold enough to start making changes.

THIS is where so many people make mistakes that make the bad situation of a divorce even worse. Read on for mistake proofing at the next stage of the process.

CHAPTER 8

GET ME OUTTA HERE!

"I knew something I did got me in this huge mess of a marriage, so something had to change. I set out to change almost everything in my life. It was the '70s, and I was no longer going to be the housewife from 'Leave it to Beaver,' so I decided I was going to be the personification of Helen Reddy's 'I am Woman Hear Me Roar.' I moved to a different side of the state, I created a new career, I dated lots of people, and I even changed my hair. I changed nearly everything I could think of. It took years to finally realize it, but after everything had changed, I realized I was left with me. I was in a new city with a new career, a new boyfriend, and a new hairstyle but something still wasn't right. I was still there, unchanged." – E.H.

HOW TO DIVORCE WELL

We can learn a lot from this woman's story. We can make good decisions after a year or two, but not typically during the initial stages of a separation and divorce. It's traumatic. It's not the time to make any unnecessary decisions that lead to big changes.

- "But everywhere I turn in my home is a bad memory. I want to move!"
- "But everyone at church knows my business. I feel so exposed."
- "But I'm feeling stuck and in pain. I need a change of scenery, or it feels like it's all going to happen all over again."
- "I'm so lonely."

At some point, we need to make changes. In fact, some changes are necessary, inevitable, and part of the actual divorce process right at the beginning. However, this is exactly the reason to avoid additional unnecessary changes. Divorce, by nature, brings on physical, emotional, and mental stress. Our lives radically change. We are closing a chapter. Making unnecessary changes in significant areas is like trying to make a new foundation based on moving sand.

> Making unnecessary changes in significant areas is like trying to make a new foundation based on moving sand.
> #HowToDivorceWell

WHEN DO I MAKE CHANGES?

That's a great question, but first I'd ask you, "What changes do you have control of and what are things completely out of your control?"

Next, I'd ask, "What changes are going to have the greatest impact on you?"

And then I'd follow it up with, "What is most important to you as you envision yourself coming out on the other side of divorce?"

Here are some areas of change I ask my clients about.

Not everything is in our control during a divorce. Circle below the areas YOU DO have control of whether it changes/happens or not:

- Church
- New gym/exercise routine
- Last name change (women)
- Savings/Retirement Plan
- Home
- New hobby
- New person in your love life
- New social life (new friend circles, new social activities)
- School/Attending New Training
- Local services (cleaners, bank, doctors, etc.)
- Job (new job in the same field where you're currently employed)
- Hair cut/color
- Neighborhood/Community
- Career (different than job, new career path)

HOW TO DIVORCE WELL

For parents, more areas are included in my follow-up book, "How to Divorce Well for Parents".

Keys I found that worked:

KEY #1 Big long-term impact = Make decisions slowly. (as much as it was in my control).
   Examples: Changing career or moving.
KEY #2 Small long-term impact = Make those decisions with ease and go for it!
   Examples: Hair cut or new hobby.

Divorce has been likened to trying to pull apart two pieces of paper that are glued together. Once ripped apart, both pieces of paper are going to be torn and need to go through the mending process individually. I'll speak for myself. In retrospect, during the first couple of years of the divorce, I wasn't thinking clearly. Even the people I would've considered dating then, I would not consider dating today – not because they have changed, but because I have. I have grown and developed. You are growing and developing. I'm now making different – I would say better – decisions because I'm a more authentic, truer version of myself. I've mended and healed, but it took time and effort.

> Even the people I would've considered dating then, I would not consider dating today – not because they have changed, but because I have.
> #HowToDivorceWell

Like many of my clients, in the middle of my divorce I was dealing with a lot of uncertainty and fear. This really rings true to me:

> "It doesn't pay to worry, but it does cost us to worry. Many bad decisions can be traced back to a response to fear."
> - Pastor Robert Jeffress

I didn't want to make decisions out of fear. Things I had very little control over, I had to accept. I turned my attention to areas I could control. What many clients have told me is their regret for making rash decisions based on feelings. So, in answer to your very good question, "When do I make changes," my answer is "it depends."

The problem is, we don't know what we don't know.

We don't know we'll regret something – or else we wouldn't do it, right? So how do we make better decisions? Now that, my friend, is a very good question, and one much easier to answer.

> My pride was the only thing keeping my head above water and I wouldn't have been able to admit I wasn't competent...
> #HowToDivorceWell

As my girlfriend says, our goal after divorce is to be living, "awake, aware and alive!" Those are three adjectives that did NOT describe me the first couple of years after the divorce. I probably wouldn't have been able to admit it because my pride was the only thing keeping my head above water and I wouldn't have been able to admit I wasn't competent... but truth be told, I was operating as only a fraction of myself. Don't be discouraged, though. You're on your way. The point is we just need to be slow and cautious with major decisions.

HOW TO DIVORCE WELL

I know the biblical truth perfectly exemplified what I would've been doing had I made big decisions during that first two years:

> "... *he who hurries with his feet*
> *[acting impulsively and proceeding without*
> *caution or analyzing the consequences]*
> *misses the mark."*
> (Proverbs 19:2b AMP)

Said another way,

> *"If you are too eager, you will miss the road...*
> *rushing feet make mistakes."*
> (Proverbs 19:2b CEV)

Referring back to E.H.'s experience at the beginning of this chapter, acting impulsively, proceeding without caution or analyzing the consequences made her miss the mark. She would say her rushing feet did make mistakes, mistakes she regretted for many years to come.

E.H. now says,

> "I made the years after my divorce worse than they needed to be. My divorce was only the beginning of the painful years to come. My now adult children would say that the decisions I made AFTER the divorce were more to blame for the painful relationship I have with them to this day.
>
> Whoever was 'to blame' in the divorce doesn't matter as much to them as the way they felt their lives were

shattered following the break-up with their dad. I was hurt, I was young, and I didn't have a role model. I was acting selfishly, and I wish I would've done things differently. I wouldn't have moved so much, dated so much, or even changed careers. I really didn't need any of that. I was just hurting. They needed a stable mom. I wasn't that for them. That's one of the greatest regrets of my life."

She further explains the repair of the relationship with her children took decades.

Once the smoke clears and we've made it through the first couple of years, we have a stronger foundation. That's our goal. I needed to slow down and regain some stability. We'll get there. Keep reading...

So, going back to your original question, "When do I make changes?" here's the general rule: If we've been married for 10 years, take at least a year to make changes. If we've been married for 20, take two years to make big changes – basically a year for every decade together. I was told to do whatever I could do to not make significant changes in the initial stages.

"I REALLY WANT TO DATE! Actually, I already am, but I'm not going to tell you!"

I get it. We're suddenly alone when we're used to having a partner. We've been hurt, and it feels good when someone new tells us they like us, wants to spend time with us – for the first time in a long time we are hearing that we're worthy to be liked. I really get it.

HOW TO DIVORCE WELL

The problem comes because dating too soon can often create more problems than we started with.

Top three reasons to wait to date.

1. **For starters, let's look at why we're dating.**
   Many of us want to do something new to avoid our pain. In the long run, it doesn't help. We can't just "get over it." We can't go around it. Eventually we need to go *through* it. Postponing the pain just makes it compound itself within us, and it's just like compound interest on a loan, it makes the original situation worse, and worse, and worse.

2. **When we're first coming out of a relationship, our "pickers" are off.**
   If we start dating immediately, it's likely that we will select the same type of person we are married to – even though they may seem completely different, and we think that they're different at the time.

   A friend said she later realized the guy she was dating was, "Just a different costume but the same monster of my ex-husband. He was so charming at the beginning, but he degrades me just like my ex did. How do I keep choosing the same type of man?"

   We tend to choose what is comfortable and what we're used to – completely unconsciously. "It feels like we've known each other our whole lives…" can often be because we have a missing piece in ourselves that our ex filled. That feeling of familiarity be it good or bad can bring about the subconscious feeling of comfort

GET ME OUTTA HERE!

for us. Instead this is a great opportunity to "date ourselves" and learn about ourselves so we don't live an emotional groundhog day.

> This is a great opportunity to "date ourselves" and learn about ourselves so we don't live an emotional groundhog day
> #HowToDivorceWell

3. **High failure rate.**

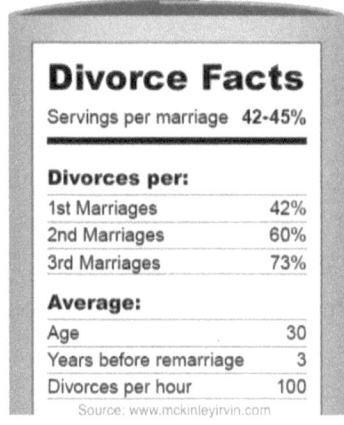

Another study in 2019 study reported by Dallas Whole Life Counseling of Plano, TX reflects an even worse outlook:

1st Marriage – 50% Divorce
2nd Marriage – 67% Divorce
3rd Marriage – 72% Divorce

Studies show that second marriages and third marriages have an even higher divorce rate than first marriages. In my experience, I am not the same person I was at the beginning of my divorce after having gone through the five stages I've shared with you in this book:

HOW TO DIVORCE WELL

- Wake-up/Shock
- Triage/Prioritize
- Breathe/Stabilize
- Make yourself marketable
- Launch the 2.0 version of your life

I would argue that I would choose a partner differently today than I would have before I went through the five stages of healing. Because when the divorce first started, I had not yet given myself time to breathe, gotten to know myself as an individual, and become healthy to make choices as a thriving, independent woman.

Who wins? For those who do take the time to heal, self-reflect, take responsibility for our own part, learn, grow, and develop to better ourselves, we're more likely to end up in healthy relationships following our divorce.

"MY DAILY ROUTINE JUST BRINGS BACK OLD MEMORIES!"

Yes, it can, but it doesn't mean it's bad. It may still serve us. If it wasn't something we eliminated in Chapter 5 when we cut out the negative influences, as much as possible, try to keep your daily routine the same. If you are used to going to the gym regularly, don't stop. If you're used to getting together with friends on Wednesday night, don't stop. If you're used to going to bed at a certain time, even if you wake up 10 times throughout the night, do it. The goal is to try to create predictability in our surroundings. It will serve you well when the inevitable, unexpected chaos comes across our paths.

"BUT I NEED TO CHANGE CAREERS!"

If you have to change careers, try to do something close to the career you are currently in. You have the most contacts there. You have the most networking prospects from your current career and it's likely where you have the most knowledge and experience. It may not be what you ultimately want to do, but it limits the amount of change you need to experience. It's a comfortable environment, like putting on an old shoe.

What if I need to change careers because we work together?

Did you work together or co-own a business? I get it. At least initially, try to stay in the same industry. People know you in that industry and will try to help you as they know that you're going through something difficult. This was my case. I contacted and networked with my friends to get my resume out as soon as possible. In the beginning I tried to do small jobs that required very little mental effort, and I was able to use that time to get my resume out to people who could help me find a position in my new career.

"WHY STAY IN OUR HOME IF IT HAS BAD MEMORIES?"

Again, we're trying to minimize the change in our lives and our circumstances. We have enough chaos and change happening out of our control in the divorce. Divorce can bring trauma, fear, anger, and a myriad of emotions. Guess what stresses come with moving? Finding a new home, making a down payment, finding movers, sorting, and packing, address changes for all the companies you deal with... just to name a few. We don't need to add more stress to an already stressful time, unless absolutely necessary.

MOVING = STRESS

What are some positive reasons for staying in the same home? We're trying to minimize change in our lives and our surroundings: our doctors, cleaners, hairstylist, church, local market, neighbors, friends, etc.

If you can't afford to stay in the home, try to get a smaller house or an apartment in the same neighborhood. When you stay in the same area, you have the same resources, including your parents, family, and friends.

MOVING = STRESS
#HowToDivorceWell

WHAT ARE THE BENEFITS OF MINIMIZING UNNECESSARY CHANGE?

Excellent question! Time allows us to gain perspective. If we jump right into another home, another career, or another relationship, we often times don't have a chance to gain a new perspective. We didn't give our time to find out...

- What is my life like alone?
- Can I really survive?
- Am I able to be independent?

GET ME OUTTA HERE!

For some of us, that's a big revelation at the beginning. Others feel like they've been living alone for years of their marriage. Either way, we need to learn to make decisions for ourselves as a single person. We need to learn to live with ourselves.

What does it look like to do this right?
What is in your control? Some things may not be in your control. Whatever is in your control, don't go changing.

LET'S PUT IT TO WORK!

Remember our list at the beginning of this chapter? You circled what you do have control of whether or not it needs to change right now.

List those here:

_____

_____

_____

_____

My Challenge: Circle at least three and commit to yourself to NOT changing them – And for who? YOU!

Although we *think* we might be thinking clearly right now, the consistent story I hear from clients and friends is that they look back and regret the decisions made early on, as they came out of a place of anger, sadness or loneliness.

I wanted to make decisions out of happiness, self-confidence, feeling fulfilled and full of joy moving forward into the next chapter. There's a difference between making a decision out of weakness or out of strength.

> "There's a difference between making a decision out of weakness or out of strength."
> #HowToDivorceWell

We have nothing to lose by taking our time.

> NOW IS YOUR GREATEST MOMENT OF POWER!
> #HowToDivorceWell

Think about what you have control of right now. NOW IS YOUR GREATEST MOMENT OF POWER! If you slow down, give yourself time to think, and not add anything more to your plate, you'll be empowered to make better decisions. You'll thank yourself for later.

I hope you'll join me and do yourself that favor.

CHAPTER 9

WHAT DO I TELL PEOPLE?

When I'm socializing, it's so hard...

"I feel like I'm walking around with a neon sign on my forehead, 'I'm divorced. I'm a failure. I've been rejected. I have baggage in my past.'"

"I feel like people think I should've seen the red flags. I should've chosen differently. I shouldn't have gotten fat, etc."

"I feel like a failure! I couldn't make it work. I couldn't make them _____ (FILL IN THE BLANK: love me, stay with me, stay faithful, keep our family together, choose their addiction over me, etc.)

"Divorce feels like the scarlet letter."

HOW CAN I MOVE FORWARD IF MY DIVORCE KEEPS COMING UP IN CONVERSATIONS?

Once again, great question! If we don't have talking points about our ex, it's natural to answer with whatever is going through our minds at the time. With that strategy, we're likely to say things that might come back to hurt us.

Right now, we've got our eye on the prize, and we're getting ready to launch the 2.0 version of ourselves, right? If we keep talking about our divorce by answering leading questions like:

"How are you doing?" followed by, "How is your ex?" and then, "What is (he) doing now?" (And believe me, people will ask), we're letting others lead the narrative. Let's get some tools to help in our conversations with people outside our **3-at-3** in our **Concentric Circles.**

How do I want to define it?

Can we consider that the relationship isn't a failed relationship, but a completed relationship? Completion is positive. It gives closure and finality. It gives us clarity without anger or guilt. It also allows us to refer to that relationship from a positive perspective when being asked about our divorce or our ex.

> "It isn't a failed relationship. It's a completed relationship."
> #HowToDivorceWell

CAN WE START OUR NEXT STAGE WITHOUT COMPLETION?

Maybe there are still legal matters pending. Maybe there are still financial ties that haven't yet been severed. If the divorce is not final and there are still loose ends legally, financially, and emotionally, can we still define our former relationship with some form of finality?

Yes.

Maybe we need more time alone working on ourselves, going through the stages of wake-up, triage, breathing, and then reinventing ourselves to thrive. Maybe we need more time working on self-care, working through pain and anger with our 3-at-3, developing and enforcing boundaries, or working through anger and pain in therapy. In other words, time and healing. That's okay.

We can still define our former relationship with finality.

The more confidence and clarity we have in the finality of our marriage, the easier we're able to move forward. In the above circumstances, people can still move ahead.

WHAT DOES IT LOOK LIKE TO MOVE FORWARD WITHOUT COMPLETION?

For examples of people who have moved forward before they were ready, all we need to do is look on the internet for unresolved anger and passive-aggressive comments on the subject.

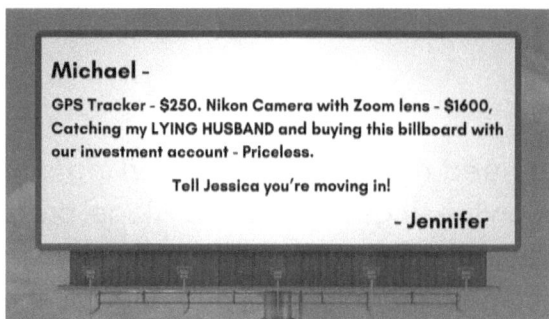

As tempting as it may be, this negative mindset taps into a "so there" attitude or feelings of revenge/hurt/anger/resentment. I don't know about you, but rehashing the negative never served me well.

"You Deserve a Break Today!"

Some of you might remember the McDonald's commercial campaign, "You Deserve a Break Today!" I was in many of those commercials. If my face looks vaguely familiar to you, it might be because many of the commercials ended with a still shot of me laughing.

WHAT DO I TELL PEOPLE?

I did a lot of commercials and tv shows growing up. In the process of auditioning and filming, I got used to memorizing scripts. That random skill served me very well in my divorce. I determined what I wanted others to know about my divorce, and I memorized talking points so I could own the narrative. I essentially wrote and memorized a script. Sounds silly, but it took a tremendous amount of pressure off me.

> I determined what I wanted others to know about my divorce, and I memorized talking points so I could own the narrative.

- I was less anxious going out in public around people we both knew.
- It built my self-esteem because I knew I wasn't talking unkindly about him.
- It kept me from constantly drudging up the negative of the past.

So, let's write your script.

WHERE DO I START?

Something that's complete has a beginning, a middle and an end, like a book or a movie. We get to write that story, so how about we say it has a happy ending? Yes, a good story has conflict, and it also has a resolution. WE get to decide how we write OUR story.

How our ex decides to write their story is of no concern to us. There are always two sides to a story. We have the opportunity to take the high road. Let's give it a shot.

HOW TO DIVORCE WELL

Let's consider naming our marriage as if we're naming a metaphorical book. What's the name of that book?

> My Horrible, Awful, No Good Time with the Dishonest Idiot Snake, Mr. Jerk. 2010-2021
> By Me

Hmmmm... maybe that's not a good title, but is that the way we often feel?

Yes.

When someone asks us how we're doing, this is our instant "go-to" response because it is how we might feel right now. I wanted to tell everyone the justification for my divorce. If I'm honest, there are still times it's tempting. However, when we spew negativity about our ex, it reflects poorly on ourselves, right? So, we have the opportunity to create a positive narrative.

LET'S PUT IT TO WORK!

YOU GET TO TAKE CONTROL OF THE NARRATIVE

This one tool has helped me more than any other to be able to talk about my ex positively versus negatively. It was especially key when speaking to those who were not my **3-at-3**. It gave me a tangible tool to practice self-control and bite my lip more easily.

So, let's start with the beginning of the book.

- What was it like when you first met? List three positive character traits that attracted you to them. What were your feelings when you first met them? There had to be a reason why we were attracted to our spouses in the first place. After all, we married them, right?

    1. _____

    2. _____

    3. _____

- Now, name three wonderful experiences or events at the beginning of the relationship. Maybe a vacation, a family gathering, a celebration, a graduation, etc.

1. _____

2. _____

3. _____

- Now, think of three wonderful things that were accomplished in the relationship. Maybe you have children. Maybe you bought your first home together. Maybe you started a business. Maybe you excelled in your career. Did either of you further your education or career path?

1. _____

2. _____

3. _____

Now we have nine adjectives, events and accomplishments that have to do with our ex in this metaphorical book. Let's close the book and, on the spine, let's name it. Let's say, my time, my accomplishments, my happy times with my ex.

NEW BOOK TITLE (example)

Having Wonderful Children, Buying a Home, and Traveling to the Maldives with my Magnanimous Husband Herbert 2010-2021

WHAT DO I TELL PEOPLE?

What's your book's title based on the nine adjectives/events you've listed above?

_____

with _____ (your ex) years _____ - _____
    By _____ (your name)

Now, when someone outside of your first two circles we discussed in the 3-at-3 chapter asks about us, this can be our response. For example:

"How are you doing?"
"There are good days and bad days, but I'm doing well. I'm grateful for the good times we had together, and all we accomplished. We bought a home, I got my master's degree, and we loved traveling. We have two amazing children together that I'm so incredibly grateful for. He really is a magnanimous guy, and I wish him well. I'm just trying to focus on my future right now."
Now, try it for yourself.

Acquaintance: "How are you doing these days? Do you ever see your ex?"
"There are good days and bad days, but I'm doing well. I'm grateful for _____ and that we accomplished _____."

We... (accomplishments)

    1. _____

HOW TO DIVORCE WELL

2. _____

3. _____

that I'm so incredibly grateful for. He really is a _____ person, and I wish him/her well. I'm just trying to focus on my future right now."

Wow. You sound confident!
Wow. You shut the questioner down!
Wow. You have control of the narrative.

Bravo!

Why does this work?

Just like a script for a commercial or tv show, the script was:

- Carefully and intentionally written.
- Written with a goal in mind of bringing the consumer or audience to a desired conclusion.

Once I memorized the "script" I wrote, I didn't have to think about it. It just came out of my mouth naturally.

> Once I memorized the "script" I wrote, I didn't have to think about it. It just came out of my mouth naturally.
> #HowToDivorceWell

Is it honest?

Yes. Is it appropriate? Yes. Are there days we don't feel like talking about it? Yes. Are there people we don't feel like talking about it with? Yes. This is our go-to response. We now have an arsenal/repertoire of responses to choose from, which will include the adjectives we pre-selected about them, the events we selected, and the accomplishments we selected.

WE control the narrative and don't need to go down the negative road. The conversation about your ex will likely end quickly as you can then start talking about what you're doing now, and what you're hoping to do in the future.

Although divorce might currently feel like it's your entire identity, and it is all you think about and deal with, it's not. Our divorce is not all that we are, and there's more to us than just our divorce. If the metaphorical "book" we create is a huge neon sign on our forehead, let's decide what it says about us and our past. We get to write the script and book title.

ARE WE IN DENIAL THAT THE RELATIONSHIP WENT BAD?

No, of course not, but we're in control of the story. We're taking control of our environment by not feeding people any additional negative information or constantly rehashing the negative.

Do those negative parts exist? Absolutely. Are we denying that there are negative parts? Absolutely not. That's for a counseling session or our 3-at-3.

Mother Teresa said, "Some people come into our lives as a blessing. Some come into our lives as a lesson." Some are both. Some came in as a blessing and left as a lesson. However, we look at it, we benefit from taking the lesson from the relationship. What did we learn? What will we do differently next time? What led to the failure of the relationship? What was our part? What can we do differently next time? All of those are positives to take away from the marriage we're leaving. Leave with a lesson.

> "Some people come into our lives as a blessing. Some come into our lives as a lesson."
> #HowToDivorceWell

As Nelson Mandela famously said, "I never lose. I either win or I learn."

Mistakes and consequences can be the best teachers in life.

Still having a hard time coming up with positive adjectives about your ex or your time together?

Look at old Instagram, Facebook, or photograph albums. While wandering down memory lane, I like to just keep using that muscle of forgiveness. I have to remind myself that forgiveness isn't a feeling, but an action. As I go through the photos and memories, I forgive both my ex and myself.

I want to throw the book in the trash!

While on the topic of social media, I've noticed some people have gone through and deleted all photos of their ex. I did not do this. I see that time as a chapter in my life. I'm not denying it happened nor attempting to hide it. It's part of my past, and it's just that – the past.

In fact, most times when I'm referring to my ex, I call him my "former husband." Just that change alone sets a different tone. Calling him my "ex" feels like it's almost x-ing him out, or that time of my life. We have two incredible kids together. I wouldn't trade anything in the world for them. So just that alone makes me incredibly grateful for that time in my life.

> "...most times when I'm referring to my ex, I call him my 'former husband.'"
>
> #HowToDivorceWell

The metaphorical book, just like the relationship, is not thrown in the trash or flushed down the toilet. It existed. It still exists. It's a book. It's a time in our lives.

Where do I keep those memories?

That book is left on the shelf. And when we look or walk by it, we don't have to constantly rehash bad memories. It can be named nicely. It reads sideways and vertically so we don't really read it too easily or often, right?

We only see the book when someone brings it up, or we happen to walk by it. Anger might pass each time we walk by it, but that anger could be a trigger to pray. Pray to forgive them and ourselves.

Now, if we have written on the book spine a title with good moments and put it on the shelf, it reminds us it's CLOSED. It allows us to move forward with completion.

Now it's YOUR time!

It's time for you to start our new book. Forgive them, forgive yourself and move on to a new chapter of YOUR lives. Here's how many of us did it in the upcoming chapters!

CHAPTER 10

OOOOH! HOW EXCITING!

> *"We can't become what we need to be by remaining what we are."*
> — **Oprah Winfrey**

YOU'RE HERE!

IT'S TIME TO LAUNCH SEQUENCE FOR THE 2.0 VERSION OF YOU AND YOUR NEW LIFE!

You've gained a strong foundation as you've **triaged**, and you're continuing to care for yourself as you **breathe**. You're probably now starting to catch a glimmer of hope as you're

HOW TO DIVORCE WELL

feeling **stabilized** and even started to venture off into the brave new world to **market yourself** in both your career and personal life as you realize you're now controlling the narrative around your divorce. You've acknowledged it's not a failed relationship, it's a completed one, and you've titled your divorce story and set it on the shelf – LET'S GO!

10 – 9 – 8 – 7 – 6 –

Can you feel it? The ground is rumbling as the fire ignites the rocket boosters under you.

It's shaky!

It feels unstable!

That's normal. We're getting ready for lift off and it can feel a little rocky. New beginnings can feel that way. Maybe you can relate to how I started. I was more than shaky and unstable – I felt like a complete mess!

What do you do when you need to clean out and organize your closet?

Do you carefully go through each piece, try on each item you haven't worn in a while and place it in its proper new place? Wow! That's amazing.

I don't. It feels like a messy process.

OOOOH! HOW EXCITING!

I pull out every single piece, throw it on my bed in huge stacks. Then I look at my empty closet and clean out all the dust bunnies in the corners, decide on new organization systems and containers, and turn to the mess that's on my bed and sort through everything piece by piece. Some things I keep, some I give away, and some I toss.

By the end of the day, I look at the closet and I'm so thrilled with the clean, organized space I've created. Boy, do I sleep well. When I embark on a new project, I start by accepting the fact it might get a bit messy before it's organized and I'm at peace. Can you relate?

> "When I embark on a new project, I start by accepting the fact it might get a bit messy before it's organized and I'm at peace."
> #HowToDivorceWell

HOW DO I FIGURE OUT WHAT I WANT IN MY NEXT CHAPTER?

Much like sorting out our closets, today we're sorting out our new lives. How did I create a clean, organized closet? It was a process. The process started out messy. Messy is how it felt when trying many jobs/careers after my marriage fell apart. In my efforts to "not go changing," one thing that had to change for me was my career/job. I'm now doing my dream job while I write and speak around the country and living a very fulfilled life. I love my life.

How did I get here? I drove Uber, worked with vacation rentals, sold medical supplies, was a background actor on

HOW TO DIVORCE WELL

TV shows, drove Uber, worked at an interior design store, sold tile and stone, was a personal assistant… Oh, did I mention? I drove for Uber.

Yup. It was messy. It was also humbling. I tried many, many different jobs and career paths to figure out what would be ideal.

Please don't let that scare you. It may sound overwhelming to read all at once, but it all happened exactly as it should have… and it will for YOU too! God led me every step of the way… and He will for YOU too!

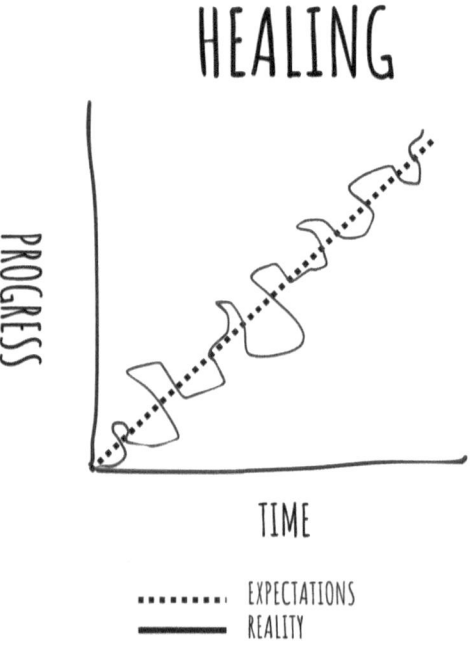

The journey wasn't a straight path. This pretty much sums up what I thought it would be like and what it was actually like.

OOOOH! HOW EXCITING!

Most of us will have similar paths.

If we asked King Solomon for wisdom, he would remind us: "Plant your seed in the morning and keep busy all afternoon, for you don't know if profit will come from **one activity or another – or maybe both**." (Ecclesiastes 11:6 NLT)

What am I suggesting?

Plant many seeds and keep busy all afternoon because you don't know if you'll profit from **one activity or another – or maybe both**. This is a time we get to try new things in our lives. Looking back on your list of things in your "Get Me Outta Here!" chapter, what needs to change? Your housing situation? Your job? Your retirement goals? Your spare time activities that no longer include your ex? That extra time, energy, and opportunity to focus on 2.0 you is exciting!

WHERE DO I START?

Now is the time when we have an empty spot in our lives. We get to explore new avenues we haven't explored before. We get to see what we're good at and experience new things that might be a fit for us, so we move on. When we try new places, hobbies, and jobs, we meet new people who might lead us to our next opportunity. In the process, we find out what we like and don't like. Now that we're single, the things we liked when we were married may not be the same activities and places we enjoy now. We get to see what we want and what we don't. Keep mental notes or a journal and you'll see patterns emerge.

HOW TO DIVORCE WELL

Here are some ideas:

- Research new career/job options.
- Join a gym.
- Meet up with longtime friends.
- Volunteer.
- Take up a new sport (golf, pickleball, cycling, hiking).
- Home/living situation (consider a roommate?).
- Daily routine (switch up the order you do things in the morning).
- Ladies: Change your last name.
- Buy a new bed (or mattress… or at least bedsheets!).
- Unfriend and unfollow your ex from all social media. If you need to know about it, your friends will tell you whether you want to know or not. (I found this to work 100% of the time).
- Try out a new clothing style.
- Take a random day off of work.
- Develop a new evening routine to calm and take care of yourself.
- Redecorate the house, a room, or at least move around the furniture.
- Listen to a new music station or a station you listened to during another era (i.e. the '80s or '90s).
- Reach out to someone in your work environment or industry who intimidates you and ask to meet up.
- Book a photo session for headshots. Get a makeover ahead of time.
- Try a new hair cut or color. Try new make-up or lipstick first, then build up to a new hairstyle or color.
- Escape into a great book.
- Visit a different type of therapist (i.e. Cognitive Behavioral Therapy, Dialectical Behavioral Therapy,

OOOOH! HOW EXCITING!

Play Therapy, Eye Movement Desensitization and Reprocessing, Acceptance and Commitment Therapy, Animal-Assisted Therapy, Applied Behavior Analysis, Attachment-Based Therapy, Bibliotherapy, Brain Stimulation Therapy, etc.).
- Take yourself out on a date. Go to a movie alone, a restaurant for dinner alone, at least sit at a coffee shop by yourself.
- Burn a new scented candle such as "beach" or "mountain" – a scent of a destination you enjoy.
- Change your make-up. Go get a makeover by your favorite cosmetics counter.
- Make an appointment with a financial advisor and consider some new financial goals for savings/investments.
- Toss everything about your ex… in a box. Give sentimental items to a friend to keep for you.
- Switch up your exercise routine. Join a partner dance class. Try a boxing class.
Exercise = endorphins = happiness.
- Take walks. Get outside. Fresh air gives a fresh perspective.
- Get a new pet (dog, cat, hamster… at least a fish!). Name it something silly.
- Join a group cooking class for a type of healthy food you've been wanting to enjoy.
- Take a vacation to visit friends and/or family.
- _____ (*your idea*)
- _____ (*your idea*)
- _____ (*your idea*)
- _____ (*your idea*)
- _____ (*your idea*)

What I did:

- Circle two that are simple.
- Circle two that are challenging (either time, effort or financially).
- Circle two that are completely outside of your comfort zone.

I made a few post-it notes with these ideas. If you're ambitious enough, make a vision board or bucket list. The key for me was to keep them in front of my eyes.

WHAT IF I'M UNCOMFORTABLE WITH TRYING NEW THINGS?

I was too. Truthfully, I'm a creature of habit. My friends will tell you I like to go to the same restaurants, visit places that are familiar to me, and as a flight attendant, I'm known to stay back in the hotel room. I know boring, right? But the truth is, I don't like change. New things can be kind of uncomfortable and scary.

But, when I do get the courage to venture out and see new things, I have new experiences, adventures and wonderful pictures. After all, if I stayed in my hotel room, my photos in Paris would look the same as my photos in Phoenix. Now is a great time to add some new, fun memories to your photo collection!

I had to look at the benefits of new things, even when it was messy.

OOOOH! HOW EXCITING!

After going through the messy process of finding my new career, I looked back at each of those jobs and realized they taught me a lot. Each one played a small part in helping me get to where I am now. Often in life, jobs are bridges getting us to where we want to be. Let's look back at my life example of "bridge" jobs and break it down by the lessons I learned.

Vacation rentals: I did well but lacked any belief in myself that I could learn new things and be good at real estate. Lesson learned: People believed in me more than I believed in myself.

Background on TV shows: This was like putting on an old shoe. I grew up doing television commercials and dancing on TV. Yes, it was easy, and many doors opened, but I still didn't like being in the industry. Lesson learned: Even though I didn't want to stay in that industry, every "no" leads me closer to my "yes."

Sales: I really love working with people, I like to inform/teach, and I could ask for a good salary, but it wasn't a good long-term fit. Lesson learned: I now have the confidence to ask for a salary I deserve.

Personal assistant: I found out I needed to organize my own life before I tried to help someone else organize theirs. Lesson learned: The foundation of my personal life needed to be in order.

Uber/Lyft Driver: I learned my way around Los Angeles, and how to survive in the bad side of town. Lesson learned: Discovered I could do way more than I thought as I overcame intimidation of getting around a major metropolitan city.

HOW TO DIVORCE WELL

Are you fearful of new things like I was?

It's easy to be. You are not alone. Unfortunately, research shows that more than 40% of marriages end in divorce, so we can be quite certain that there are others out there just as insecure as we are who are exploring new hobbies and interests. George Adair once said, "Everything you've ever wanted is on the other side of fear. If we don't change, we can't expect new results."

I had to ask myself, what I wanted: The pain of staying where I was or the pain of growth? That's a choice that you have as well. I found a strength that comes from it. Strength didn't come from doing what I could do well. Strength came from overcoming new things I thought I couldn't. So why not try some new things? We don't need to be prisoners of our past. We can be the architects of our futures.

> "Everything you've ever wanted is on the other side of fear."
> - George Adair
> #HowToDivorceWell

> "Strength didn't come from doing what I could do well. Strength came from overcoming new things I thought I couldn't."
> #HowToDivorceWell

Are you feeling unsettled and want to make a decision, or stuck like you're in a rut?

Ask yourself these questions:

What career would I have if I had no fear? _____

OOOOH! HOW EXCITING!

What would I do if I had the "right" education/training?

_____

_____

> What did I want? The pain of staying where I was or the pain of growth?
> #HowToDivorceWell

If I could do anything, anywhere, what would I do?

_____

    Career: _____

    Hobby: _____

What would I be doing if I had no responsibilities (kids, aging parent responsibilities, etc.)

_____

If I had no worries and concerns about finances, what would I do?

_____

If I didn't care about what other people thought of me, what would I do?

_____

> **FOUR THINGS MENTALLY STRONG PEOPLE DO**
> 1. They are not victims. They don't waste time feeling sorry for themselves.
> 2. They embrace change. They welcome challenges.
> 3. They are willing to take risks.
> 4. They focus on what is within their control instead of complaining about what isn't.
> #HowToDivorceWell

GO FOR IT!

You're strong and you're a leader. As you may or may not know, leaders are made, not born.

You are strong because you are making it through this very difficult situation, and you are a leader because you are leading your own life now. Now THAT is exciting and empowering!

> "Leaders are made, not born."
> #HowToDivorceWell

"There's already too much going on. I'm already feeling out of control, and I don't want to add one more new thing."

Yes, there is a lot already going on. We've also lost something. We've lost a partner, so there is a void in our lives. Many of us go through some form of depression during divorce.

OOOOH! HOW EXCITING!

New activities that take our attention and energy can be a welcome distraction.

"New things bring uncertainty! I hate the feeling of uncertainty and chaos."

When we control the decisions of which new things we try, we control the environment. When we decide to start new things, it brings confidence as we are the CEO of our new lives.

"I'm already discouraged. I've heard too many no's and divorce itself is its own rejection."

If we decide to look at the "no"s from a different perspective, it might help. As I discovered, our "no"s bring us one step closer to our "yes." There is no better teacher and guide to our future than our past – both what we say "no" to, and what we say "yes" to.

"It's embarrassing!"

I was not only embarrassed, I was also scared. It's unsettling. Going back to the analogy of cleaning out my closet, what if a new friend dropped by to see me while I was cleaning and reorganizing? They'll see a big mess, and that's embarrassing. Ugh.

Who wants to be a grown adult and unsure about our career or other aspects of our lives? None of us. Stability can breed security and instability can breed insecurity. At times, all the change brought out horrible insecurities in myself and my self-worth.

HOW TO DIVORCE WELL

That was why it was so important to start and end every day with a gratitude list. I had already cut out people, places, and things that were negative in my life and began replacing them with new positive influences. Had I not placed positive people in my life, positive stations on the radio, and positive social media feeds, I would've likely given up and not reached my dreams.

LET'S PUT IT TO WORK!

HOW DO I START?

Try lots of different things. Let people know that you're looking to do new things via text, social media, or an old-fashioned phone call!

The area of my life I'm going to try new things (career, hobby, exercise, etc.) _____

1. Reach out to old (healthy) contacts.
People I know who are thriving/loving their _____ (same area you mentioned above - career, hobby, exercise, etc.)

Name	How I'm going to reach out (circle)
_____	Email Call Text
_____	Email Call Text
_____	Email Call Text

2. Become a member of or follow 10 new positive groups on social media. Whether it's about hiking singles in your area or a career change that you've

always wanted to make. Type in "I love to _____" to your social media and see what pops up!
3. Start following people on social media who are doing things you get excited about.
4. If it won't jeopardize a current job, put your resume out on social media. I did. That felt very vulnerable. It helped, though.
5. Find a friend who's a good photographer and go take a bunch of good pictures of yourself. Have two or three of them retouched and use that in your resume and on your social media profile. Make it your business card. This is the time to sell YOU.

One note to remember: Doing esteemable acts gives us self-esteem. So, commit to starting something new and do it – at least once. Be on time to get there – which really means early.

Seth Godin said, "If it scares you, it might be a good thing to try." Similarly, Michael Hyatt says, "More often than not, being brave means doing it scared." So, remember character is both developed and revealed by the tests that you're going through right now. It's never too late or too early to try something new.

For me, it was writing a book. I've had this book in me for more than 30 years – and I finally did it. I took small, itty-bitty, tangible steps in that direction, and I tried it. I talked to people who had written a book. This didn't just happen overnight.

P.S. If you've always wanted to write a book, list me as someone to reach out to! Just email me, and I'd love to share with you the steps and resources I used to do it!

The key:

> "If you get close to what you love,
> who you are is revealed to you."
> — Ethan Hawke

For what it's worth...it's never too late, or in my case too early, to be whoever you want to be.

There's no time limit. Start whenever you want. You can change or stay the same. There are no rules to this thing. We can make the best or the worst of it. I hope you make the best of it. I hope you see things that startle you.

I hope you feel things you never felt before. I hope you meet people who have a different point of view.

I hope you live a life you're proud of, and if you're not, I hope you have the courage to start all over again.

F. Scott Fitzgerald

There are so many options, I don't know where to start!"

Well, read on!

CHAPTER 11

GETTING' WHAT I WANT! (LASER FOCUS ON 2.0 VERSION OF YOU)

> "Look straight ahead, and fix
> your eyes on what lies before you."
> (Proverbs 4:25 NLT)

Do you find yourself...

- Staying busy all day, but your pressing priorities are not getting done?
- Trying many new things and feeling scattered?
- Having brain fog and not able to think straight or know what to do first?

HOW TO DIVORCE WELL

I did. And I felt myself...

- Not focusing on what was most important to me in the long term, the big picture.
- Reacting and responding to other people's "urgent" needs. I let other people's circumstances dictate how I was spending my time and limited energy.
- Distracted – by what, I don't know. It seemed like I was going from one "crisis" to another.
- "Spinning" and defaulting to thinking about my future fears and "what ifs".

"LASER FOCUS"

When I called him, that's what my Uncle Joe told me I needed – Laser Focus. As I sat on the beach having one of those deep, ugly, hiccup sobs, crying, "I can't do this! This is too hard!"

My calm and wise Uncle Joe in South Georgia said, "Stacey, laser focus right now. You are stronger than you think you are."

Ugh.
I didn't want to hear that.
Truth be told, I didn't believe him.... and I did not <u>want</u> to believe him.
Not only did I not feel strong, but I didn't want to have to be strong.
I was tired.

But Uncle Joe was right.

He was right because he knew when I had nowhere else to turn, I would turn to God.

GETTIN' WHAT I WANT!(LASER FOCUS ON 2.0 VERSION OF YOU)

He was right because he knew, if done right, I wasn't responsible for all my worries.

He knew God draws near to the brokenhearted, and my sobbing was evidence I was completely brokenhearted.

He knew that, "God doesn't give you more than you can handle," is nowhere in the Bible.

He knew God allows life to throw us more than we can handle.

He knew God sometimes allows us more than we can handle, because God's deepest desire is for us to rely on Him, and talk with Him. God is eager to share our struggles and pain.

Just like any good earthly father would, God wants to hear from us because He cares about us. He wants us to ask Him and lean on Him for help. He promises with Him, the burden is light.

> "My yoke is easy and my burden is light." Mt. 11:30
> #HowToDivorceWell

> "Come to me, all you who are weary and burdened, and I will give you rest. Take my yoke upon you and learn from me, for I am gentle and humble in heart, and you will find rest for your souls. For my yoke is easy and my burden is light."
> Matthew 11:28-30 (NIV)

By the way, the often-misquoted verse about not giving us more than we can handle actually says, "...God is faithful.

HOW TO DIVORCE WELL

He will not allow temptation to be more than you can stand. When you are tempted, He will show you a way out so that you can endure." 1 Corinthians 10:13b NLT

It's about temptation. God doesn't allow us to be tempted more than we can handle, which is also encouraging, but it says nothing about hardships. He will allow us to be given more hardship than we can handle.

Do you feel you have more than you can handle right now? I sure did.

> "God doesn't give you more than you can handle" is nowhere in the Bible.
> #HowToDivorceWell

And you are stronger than you think you are, too. It also wasn't what I wanted to hear because I didn't want to have to be strong. All I wanted was for someone to tell me it was all going to be okay. I wanted someone to assuage all my fears, to tell me about my new career, set up my trust fund and say, "You've been through a lot, now just take care of yourself." Nope. My Uncle Joe basically said,

"Suck it up Buttercup, you've got this!"

I was feeling anything BUT laser focused!

Can you relate to any of the following circumstances?

- Paul says we're acting like children... "Tossed to and fro by the waves and carried about by every wind..." (Ephesians 4:14 ESV) and also reminds us "The one who doubts is like a wave of the sea that is driven and tossed by the wind." (James 1:6 ESV)

GETTING' WHAT I WANT!(LASER FOCUS ON 2.0 VERSION OF YOU)

- Luke gives us an insight into someone who was focusing on multiple things and losing sight of what was most important. When Jesus was visiting Mary and Martha, Martha was distracted by the big dinner she was preparing. She came to Jesus and complained about her sister not doing the same. But the Lord corrected her, "Martha, Martha, you are anxious and troubled about many things, but one thing is necessary." (Luke 10:41-42 ESV).

In contradiction,

- Solomon says a wise person refuses to be distracted from his goal. "Let your eyes look straight ahead; fix your gaze directly before you." (Proverbs 4:25 NIV).
- Paul advises to "… be sure that everything is done properly and in order." (1 Corinthians 14:40 NLT)

How are you feeling?
I was feeling like a child being tossed to and fro… definitely not fixing my gaze on any one thing, or what was directly before me.

Like Martha, I felt anxious and troubled, not knowing how to focus on priorities. I was not getting things done properly and in order.

While every situation is unique, here are some personal examples of things someone might regret during a divorce, realizing later that they could have better focused on goals and priorities:

On the next page, circle any you might want to improve.

1. **Reacting Emotionally Instead of Strategically:** Responding impulsively to emotional situations during the divorce process, such as arguments or disagreements, instead of approaching things with a more strategic mindset.
   p.s. This book should be helping you here!
2. **Neglecting Self-Care:** Ignoring personal well-being by neglecting physical and mental health, which could harm your overall focus and productivity.
3. **Overcommitting or Isolating:** Either overcommitting to new activities to distract from the divorce or isolating yourself from social support, rather than finding a balanced approach.
4. **Engaging in Revenge Actions:** Seeking revenge or trying to hurt your ex emotionally, which may provide temporary satisfaction but can hinder long-term healing.
5. **Ignoring Legal Advice:** Disregarding legal advice or not fully understanding your rights and responsibilities, leading to unfavorable outcomes in court or during negotiations.
6. **Neglecting Financial Planning:** Failing to create a clear financial plan for the post-divorce period, resulting in financial challenges and difficulties in achieving personal goals.
7. **Losing Focus at Work:** Letting personal issues significantly impact professional life, such as neglecting work responsibilities, which could lead to professional setbacks.
8. **Not Seeking Professional Support:** Avoiding counseling or therapy to address emotional challenges and gain coping mechanisms, which can hinder personal growth and healing.

GETTING' WHAT I WANT!(LASER FOCUS ON 2.0 VERSION OF YOU)

9. **Failing to Set Clear Boundaries:** Struggling to establish clear boundaries with the ex-spouse, which may lead to ongoing conflicts and difficulties moving forward.
10. **Ignoring Children's Needs:** Not prioritizing the well-being and emotional needs of children during the divorce process, which can have long-lasting effects on their adjustment. My book, **How to Divorce Well for Parents** really helps with this challenge, and gives parents a personal individualized blue-print, written by you, to guard and protect your children in divorce.

It's important to remember that hindsight is 20/20, and everyone makes mistakes. I sure did! What's crucial is learning from these experiences and focusing on our well-being, determining our goals, and having accountability to achieve those goals so you can help prevent future regrets.

How are you feeling?
Please answer Yes or No to the following questions:
- # 1. Do you feel you know how it's going to work out? _____
- # 2. Do you have a good idea of what your life will look like in a year? _____
- # 3. Do you believe, YOU may not know, but God does know how it's going to work out, and He has your best interest in mind? Answer honestly. No one but you will see this. _____ (Maybe and kinda are sufficient answers.)
- # 4. Do you believe God can work everything together for good for those who know Him? _____
- # 5. Is that you? _____ *see the epilogue on page 229

HOW TO DIVORCE WELL

Is the answer to #3 "maybe"? Mine was.
If the answer to the last two questions is "yes," THAT is faith. THAT is trust. THAT was where the rubber meets the road with my faith, which had to become complete trust.

See God says that faith is the assurance of things hoped for, evidence of things not seen. (Hebrews 11:1 NASB)

God says all we need is faith the size of a mustard seed, which is about the size of the tip of a pen. Can you try? You can pray and ask God to give you faith. Just that little prayer is a step of faith. He can use that! If you answered "no" to questions #3 and #4, do you think you can have just a little faith... the size of a mustard seed and go back and change your answers to "yes"?

> "Faith is the assurance of things hoped for, evidence of things not yet seen."
> #HowToDivorceWell

If you can garner the amount of faith the size of a mustard seed, which is all I had at the time, you will find out, like I did, that God can be trusted, and He will give you your next steps.

What should I do next?
What I needed was to be told that I could do this and I'm stronger than I knew I was, but I needed laser focus. And if no one has told you, I will.

You can do this.
You are stronger than you think you are when you're relying on God.
You need laser focus.

GETTING' WHAT I WANT!(LASER FOCUS ON 2.0 VERSION OF YOU)

We're now entering Stage 5 and launching that 2.0 version of ourselves and our new lives. Let's not get off track! It's time to put blinders on – laser focus.

Jets are starting! Feel the ground rumbling?
That is the rumbling of something new about to take off!

"WHAT ONE THING IS NECESSARY? FOCUS ON WHAT? WHAT ORDER?"

FOCUS #1 IDENTIFY FOUNDATION:

The Priorities of your Triage

How are you doing on staying focused on your top three priorities in your triage? Basically, how are you doing at laser focusing on the bottom tiers of Maslow's Hierarchy of Needs?

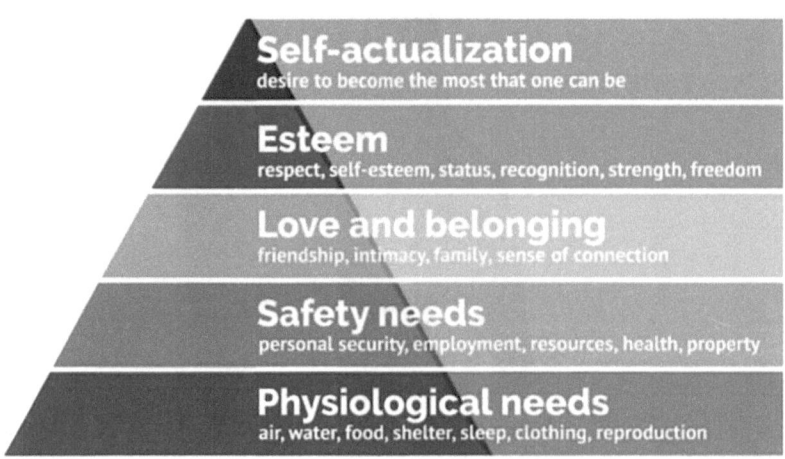

Let's remember what they are:
- I stay alive (physiological needs).
- I have a roof over my head (safety/property needs).
- I have a way to support myself (resource/employment needs).

Don't worry, in the 2.0 version of your life you'll continue to build layer upon positive layer in the hierarchy, but right now, let's make sure the foundation is solid.

GETTIN' WHAT I WANT!(LASER FOCUS ON 2.0 VERSION OF YOU)

FOCUS #2 IDENTIFY WHERE YOU'RE GOING: Vision Board

Soon after my ex and I separated, I was sharing with a friend that I had no idea what I was going to do with my career or my life. She asked me to her home to create a vision board. I had not idea what that was. "Choose a color of construction paper, and here's a stack of magazines. "Just cut out stuff that speaks to you or has any kind of meaning to you," she explained.

I didn't know anything I liked. I didn't know myself at all. I didn't think that anything had any meaning to me. But she walked away and left me standing there... alone. Me, my blue piece of construction paper, and a foot-tall stack of magazines. I figured I couldn't just turn around and walk out of her house. That wouldn't be polite.

So, for an hour I went through magazines feeling a bit childish. I cut out 15 or so pictures of things I liked.

Sure enough, she came back in exactly an hour as I apologetically explained, "I know none of these pictures make sense or have any correlation."

She looked at my picture choices and said, "What do you mean? Everything is about the same thing. It's so evident." As I stood there perplexed, she said, "That's a boat. This is water. There's a palm tree. This is sand. Stacey, didn't you grow up down in Orange County at the beach?" After I nodded, still pretty confused, she continued, "Okay, here's your assignment: Go down to walk the island where you grew up. Walk one lap around the island and drive back."

HOW TO DIVORCE WELL

That sounded so random, and had nothing to do with my problem. Yes, it was where I grew up, but what the heck did that have to do with getting me a JOB? Not to mention, at the time I lived in Pasadena and, depending on Southern California traffic, it could be anywhere from a one- to two-hour drive to where I grew up in Orange County.

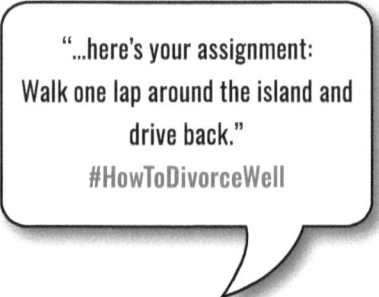

"...here's your assignment: Walk one lap around the island and drive back."
#HowToDivorceWell

But I did it.
It felt like a homework assignment, so I did it.
It felt stupid, but I did it.
I put a whole lot of miles on my darling little Prius, but I did it.

And sure enough, that gave me focus, grounded me, and allowed me to see what my next step should be. **I needed that grounding of my childhood to help me reconnect with the most authentic version of myself.** Sure enough, as I was walking the island, I ran into old childhood friends, neighborhood friends, and parents of friends that I grew up with. When I found a new church in the area, I ran into people that I had known since elementary school. Seeing those old connections helped me remember who I was.

Healing looked like this:

1. Conversations with old friends helped me remember what I liked, what I used to enjoy... my former authentic version of myself.
2. I started doing those again, and being in those places I used to like.

GETTING' WHAT I WANT!(LASER FOCUS ON 2.0 VERSION OF YOU)

3. I gradually got a sudden epiphany or inspiration for a new goal, or even the next step.
4. My next step would make it even clearer, and suddenly even goals came into view.
5. Once I determined goals, I had exactly what I needed to finally hone in and laser focus.

Is there a location you love that gives you clarity of thought?
Maybe going back to your childhood neighborhood isn't grounding or even good for you. Some people say they feel closer to God in the mountains, hiking, swimming, or surfing. Do you have a place like that?

Where is a place I feel grounded and connected to God/my authentic self/my favorite place I've lived? _____
_____

I'm going to make an appointment with myself to go visit that place on _____ (date).

Or if it takes a lot of planning:

I'm going to make a time on _____ (within the next week), to book a trip or make a plan on my calendar to go there.

What do I do when I get there?

Write. Try to dream – dream big. How?

> **Step 1:** Get a journal and spend some time dreaming. See yourself either 5 or 10 years from now. What are you doing? Where are you living? Who's in your life? Who are you impacting? Keep it at a dream crazy big

level – well call it your Dream Big Manifesto. Nothing is off the table. The book, "Living Forward" by Michael Hyatt and Daniel Harkavy was helpful for me to identify what I wanted (when I didn't even know myself again yet)... Maybe you can do it without tools. Whatever you do, make sure you dream BIG.

Step 2: Read back over your dream big manifesto and pull out 10 big goals. For me, when I did it #1 was moving back to where I grew up, #2 was writing this book. That's not to say other goals won't be in your life, but these are your biggies.

Step 3: Write down five areas of your life – spiritual, physical, social, emotional, mental. Then, under each area, write your "theme" of the goal this year (mine for spiritual is "trust & ask") and what your #1 and #2 goals are for that area.

Step 4: Write out the milestones that would occur in the next year that will get you to the above dreams/goals.

Step 5: Write weekly actions that need to occur to get you to your dreams/goals.

Bonus step: Go grab some quotes that inspire you and put them on sticky notes and your calendar. I name my years, so this year is COURAGE. So that's on a note too.

Some things will most likely shift on weekly actions or even milestones. That's why it's important to revisit them often.

GETTING' WHAT I WANT!(LASER FOCUS ON 2.0 VERSION OF YOU)

There are specific systems that guide you to do weekly planning for 20-30 minutes one day a week, and then spend 10 minutes daily planning/mapping out your week and day. I'm not quite that diligent (I'm just not wired that way), but it's a great methodology and maybe that works well for you.

This is just your initial compass and it obviously doesn't mean our dynamic God won't change the direction of our sails and priorities. It just helps us get clear.

FOCUS #3 IDENTIFY WHAT GOD'S SAYING TO DO: Don't Deny in The Darkness What He's Revealed in the Light (How to maintain your laser focus)

> *"God draws near to the brokenhearted and saves the crushed in spirit."*
> (Psalms 34:18)

This is who most of us are right now – the brokenhearted and crushed in spirit.

We've all had them – an "aha" moment – an epiphany. Expect more of them now. Why? Because God draws near to the brokenhearted. And if we are open to listen, His voice and guidance can become incredibly clear.

Can you remember the last time you had sudden clarity of thought, an intuitive idea, or known God guided you to something? Write that down.

_____

_____

Now, make a way to remind yourself of it regularly. Why? Most of us are good forgetters. After we have one of those "aha" moments, we eventually (if not immediately) start questioning ourselves. But...

> Don't deny in the darkness What He's revealed in the light.
> #HowToDivorceWell

DON'T DENY IN THE DARKNESS WHAT'S BEEN REVEALED IN THE LIGHT

What do I mean by that? If you're like me, you question, "Did I really 'hear' God?" We doubt our ability to do what we had been given sudden confidence to achieve.
Instead of doubting, hold on to those moments of clarity. Those moments are worth gold.

I found they gave me vision and confidence to take steps in the right direction when the voices of doubt inevitably crept in and gnawed away at my confidence to keep moving forward. Writing it down and keeping it visible was the key to keeping me laser focused.

"How Do I Know It's from God?"
Maybe you don't hear an audible voice. I don't. I do have a deep sense of certainty and sudden resolve that He has given me clarity. It is a deep gut feeling combined with an unexplained peace. God's voice will never tell you something that contradicts scripture, but it also may not make practical sense. As I continue to pray for clarity and next steps, I often run it by wise, trusted friends. It might be confirmed by your 3-at-3, and possibly your second concentric circle. Scripture

GETTIN' WHAT I WANT!(LASER FOCUS ON 2.0 VERSION OF YOU)

says there is wisdom in a multitude of counsel. If you have contradicting feedback, keep praying. Most often, God will give you calmness and peace that you really can't explain. If you think you've sensed something God has said, write it down (even if you're not sure):

1. _____
2. _____
3. _____

Now, pray that God would confirm it or even update it. Once you're settled, write those things somewhere you'll see them often.

"But I'm scared and I keep doubting myself!"

Me too. But this was when I think I grew up – like really entered adulthood. At least in my faith. I had a faith in God for more than 40 years, but did I really trust God? Like for my basic needs and cares? My fears?

> "To trust God in the light is nothing, but trust him in the dark- that is faith."
> C.H. SPURGEON
> #HowToDivorceWell

I found myself in a place where God allowed me to have more than I could handle. This is where the rubber met the road with my faith, where I grew feet on my faith, and had to literally just trust God.

I had to admit there was a difference for me in faith... and trust.

HOW TO DIVORCE WELL

I had faith there was a God. I had faith He existed.

Deep down, I think I had the idea that, "God helps those who help themselves." I thought the bottom line was I needed to take care of things. But that's nowhere in the Bible.

What it does say is "... cast your cares on me, for I care for you." (1 Peter 5:7)

That's why I keep reminders around me to build my confidence. As I've mentioned, I have an actual prayer card system called "The Potent Prayer Life" which some of you may have even heard of in my seminars at women's conferences. When I get moments of clarity, I write them down on cards and put them in my prayer card box. The prayer card system is a simple way that I continually remind myself of God's specific personal guidance in my journey.

> "God helps those who help themselves."
> But that's nowhere in the Bible.
> #HowToDivorceWell

Being reminded of it weekly helps keep me focused and gives me hope. Then for days I doubt (not if, but when), I remind myself to not deny in the darkness (moments of doubt) what God has revealed in the light (moments of clarity). We can't deny the feelings of doubt, but we can tell ourselves logically, exactly what was revealed in a moment God spoke.

> "Faith and fear cannot co-exist"
> #HowToDivorceWell

FOCUS #4 IDENTIFY LOOSE ENDS: What If I Forget Something?

So, we've figured out to focus on

1. Our Triage
2. Our Vision Board
3. What God has Revealed in the Light so we Don't Deny it in the Darkness

How do we know for sure we haven't forgotten anything?

Here's how we catch anything else we've missed – trust that God will reveal it to you at the right time.

Fortunately, He promises He won't leave you or forsake you.

Unfortunately, He might bring something to mind in the middle of the night when your thoughts from the day have finally quieted down. Many people find it helps to keep something to write on next to their bed for just this reason.

Remember, God draws near to the brokenhearted. This is when you can lean into God to trust He's going to help you have all your bases covered. He's our partner in this process. We are not alone.

Now what do I do after He brings something to mind and I've written it down?

Don't forget that thought. That's a great question, and it's what we'll cover in the next chapter, but while we're thinking about it, start with Step 1:

HOW TO DIVORCE WELL

Step 1. What woke me up at 3am in complete fear?

_____

Steps 2-5 We cover it in Chapter 12.

p.s. You're doing great! When we laser focus, we get more done. The negative chaos falls behind us faster, and we're more easily able to start our new lives.

"Just remember, if the way were known to you if you could handle it in your strength and wisdom – this would not be a step of faith for you. It would carry no potential for revealing the Father's character, love, power, and wisdom in your life.

So whatever God is challenging you to do, remember He will employ the full power of heaven to ensure you are able to triumph in it. Your responsibility is simply to seek, trust, and obey Him as He directs you."
– Charles Stanley
"In His Presence"

"Make your dreams tomorrow's reality." Stephen Covey

CHAPTER 12

"CELEBRATE GOOD TIMES, COME ON!"

> *"A year from now you may wish you had started today."*
> —**Karen Lamb**

Do you ever find yourself saying...

"There's too much to do! These tasks feel insurmountable."

"Even when I get something done, there are 40 more things to get done!"

"I still wake up at 3am feeling overwhelmed!"

HOW TO DIVORCE WELL

What is something on your laser focus that feels overwhelming, but you know you want to accomplish in your next chapter? Choose something that might feel intimidating or like the work it would require seems daunting.

_____

What is something outside your comfort zone you listed in Chapter 10, "Ooooh! How Exciting!" (pp. 114– 115)

_____

What is something you want to implement as a new part of your daily routine?

_____

It's true – a lot needs to get done.
It's true – procrastinating is easy.
It's true – it is overwhelming.

GOOD NEWS!

The launch sequence has been completed and you're taking off! You're breaking through the atmosphere! It's time to CELEBRATE!

Why am I feeling shaky and unstable?

Astronauts and astrophysicists will tell you that breaking through the atmosphere is the most unstable and dangerous time on the mission.

"CELEBRATE GOOD TIMES, COME ON!"

That's what we're feeling at this stage. The instability of breaking through an atmosphere. We're scared. There's a lot ahead of us, and it's easy to feel defeated and want to give up.

You've done so much work to this point – it's no time to give up! The key is to aim high but take baby steps toward those big goals.

HOW TO DIVORCE WELL

Just like what Ezekiel said:

"*Zerubbabel started rebuilding this Temple and he will complete it. That will be your confirmation that God-of-the-Angel-Armies sent me to you.* **Does anyone dare despise this day of small beginnings?** *They'll change their tune when they see Zerubbabel setting the last stone in place!*"
(Zechariah 4:10 MSG)

> "The key is to aim high, but take baby steps toward those big goals."
> #HowToDivorceWell

"What do I do when I'm feeling shaky and unstable?"

I'll give you an example:

Step 1. What woke me up at 3am in complete fear? I wrote that down.

Step 2. I considered that issue as a priority focus for the next day.

Step 3. If I still couldn't sleep, I broke that one issue into the steps that I had control over. For instance: Is there more information I can obtain? What can I do to get that information?

I then broke that first step into at least five smaller steps to make that first step even easier.

Step 4. I wrote in my calendar to do one itty-bitty, small step toward that priority (a text, an email to

"CELEBRATE GOOD TIMES, COME ON!"

that intimidating company, a reminder on my planner to send a message in the morning).

Step 5. I went back to sleep.

WHAT IT LOOKED LIKE FOR ME:

When my husband and I separated I suddenly found myself with an overwhelming load of business and financial issues to deal with that I was previously unaware of. The mere thought of the amount of work it would take to get caught up completely immobilized me. (FYI on a side note: 100% my fault for not being more involved in the finances in our marriage and business, by the way.) But I was plagued with consistent reminders I needed to deal with it, thanks to the constant stream of mail I was receiving. I would feel my heart beat so fast when I looked at the mounting stack of paperwork, I'd just have a glass of wine (or 6!) to "take the edge off," in hopes I'd come up with some magical solution in my state of relaxed, higher consciousness.

Ummm… that didn't work too well.

The paperwork was still there the next morning only now I had a headache, no new magical solutions, and I'd anticipate even more mail that day.

One day, I decided I was just going to pull out the whole stack. I did nothing more than the single action of pulling it out and taking it out where I could see it. At the end of that day, I wrote on my gratitude list: "I pulled out the stack."

Did I open a single envelope? No.
Did I look at any of them? No.
Did I organize them even by which category they were in? No.
But was I able to put something on my gratitude list? Yes.

I got them all out and they're all stacked up.
Thank you very much, take a bow.

THE GOAL?

The goal is not to solve something that feels overwhelming in a day.

This is what I found: When I freaked out about a big, overwhelming issue, I would ruminate about the worst-case scenarios playing out in the future. In actuality, it took my focus off of today, thus what I could do that day.

The truth is, I have survived 100% of the things I worried about, but never happened.

So often I want a floodlight to show me what's ahead so I can prepare. I find what God does give me is a flashlight... just enough to see what I need to do today. In fact, some days it feels like He only gives me a match... enough to see what I'm supposed to do in that moment.

> "I have survived 100% of the things I worried about, but never happened."
> #HowToDivorceWell

"CELEBRATE GOOD TIMES, COME ON!"

It reminds me that even though I want to know how things will play out, and I want assurance that everything is going to be okay, God promises us only peace for today.

> "...some days it feels like He only gives me a match worth of light on my path... enough to see what I'm supposed to do in that moment."
> #HowToDivorceWell

2 Corinthians 3:17 says, "Now the Lord is the Spirit, and where the Spirit of the Lord is, there is freedom." (NIV)

> Do you have fears about how it will work out in the future, like I did?
> Does it say, "... where the Spirit of the Lord is, there **will be** freedom?" Nope. But I was trying to have peace for the future. God's Spirit wasn't giving me peace for the future.
>
> It does say, "... where the Spirit of the Lord is, there **IS** freedom."

The goal is to take one or two simple steps we have control over. Try it. You'll be amazed at how good you'll feel after taking action on the smallest of steps... even if God only gives you a match flickering bit of light at your feet.

The importance of smaller steps

There were times I was so scared to make phone calls about the bills, I would intentionally make calls when a company was closed because I didn't have the courage to talk to a human being. I would leave a message. That was my big win for the day. It's been said that it doesn't matter how slow you go, as long as you don't stop! Celebrate those baby step wins.

LET'S PUT IT TO WORK!

Your turn (you knew it was coming!)

What is something overwhelming that you know you want to accomplish in your next chapter?

_____

I'll give you an example. What about opening your own bank account?

It was recommended to me to go to a credit union or a different bank than where we banked as a couple. I opened an account at a credit union with $25. Here were the steps I took:

1. Look online for the hours they're open.
2. Call credit union or look online for minimum deposit required.
3. Withdraw $25 cash for the deposit.
4. Make an appointment to open an account.
5. Go to the credit union.

"CELEBRATE GOOD TIMES, COME ON!"

Could we just go to the credit union and do all those things in one step? Yes, but it would've stayed on my to-do list for weeks if I had it on my list as "open account at a credit union." When it was broken down into those manageable steps, I was able to tackle it and have each step on my gratitude list each day.

> But it would've stayed on my to-do list for weeks if I had it on my list as "open account at a credit union."
> #HowToDivorceWell

Back to you.

List five steps it will take to get the "overwhelming" goal done you wrote above.

1. _____

2. _____

3. _____

4. _____

5. _____

Now, take Step 1 and break it down into the smallest steps you possibly can, such as, "1. Open the computer." Your turn:

HOW TO DIVORCE WELL

1. _____

2. _____

3. _____

4. _____

5. _____

6. _____

7. _____

8. _____

YOU CAN DO IT – BABY STEPS WORK!

Using baby steps like these, I've helped my kids apply for 30 different universities, created a website, survived major surgery, secured my own health insurance for the surgery regarding my cancer scare, applied for unemployment (which I never thought I would do – I was mortified!), moved out of our home of 14 years, survived five Christmases I planned, pulled-off nine birthday parties for my kids, had a dented car insured, gotten my car repaired, bought a new car, got both kids insured and driving, developed solid credit, started a new career, moved to my dream neighborhood, secured a financial advisor, wrote a book, and secured speaking engagements and launched a thriving coaching and consulting business. I did each one of those things using baby steps.

YOU CAN DO IT!

It's easy to feel like not a lot is getting done.

It's important to remember what you've done so you can see progress. No matter how small the accomplishments may be, put each one of your successes on an index card and tape it somewhere you'll see regularly like the inside of a medicine cabinet. Keep adding to it. Remind yourself when you're overwhelmed or discouraged – you are progressing!

List of things I've already accomplished:

1. _____

2. _____

3. _____

4. _____

5. _____

6. Now, keep that list going! I keep mine on an index card.

I keep this index card in my prayer cards, so I read the list of all I've accomplished every week. It inevitably comes up at the perfect time when I'm overwhelmed or intimidated by a new daunting task. I can remember what I have been able to accomplish before, and it gives me the courage to take baby steps toward the next major project.

No step is too small except taking no step at all.

What if taking such small steps feels stupid?
Get over it. You are not alone. It's normal to want things to move faster than they do but Rome wasn't built in a day. It was built one brick at a time. Just start! Author John C. Maxwell once said, "Have you ever met a successful person who quit his or her way to the top? You can't win if you don't stay in the game, right? By taking small baby steps, we stay in the game."

Remember the items you listed in your self-care section of Breathe?
When you get even the smallest of baby steps, do something celebratory. Do a little crazy dance. Have a glass of wine. I do jumping jacks. I put on a favorite song from the 1980s and dance disco by myself. Maybe you go get your nails done. Maybe you get a little extra massage with your pedicure. Maybe you watch some sports. Maybe you go golfing. Google ideas of how to celebrate small successes, and spoil yourself. You can't afford it? Low on cash? You surely can afford a crazy dance and a bubble bath!

"CELEBRATE GOOD TIMES, COME ON!"

Keep a list of little ways to celebrate. I often choose one before I start a project.

> For example: "If I complete texts to the three people I want to ask to be references on my resume, I will get an extended foot massage at my pedicure."

Celebrations are tiny but important ways to congratulate ourselves. They inspire us to keep going. They are important.

What's something small you can do for yourself this week after accomplishing one of your baby steps? _____
_____

Well, final edit of Chapter 12 is done, so I'm taking my own advice. I'm heading out for a 10-minute walk around the block after a good set of jumping jacks.

Love you guys! See you soon to wrap it all up together!
S.

HOW TO DIVORCE WELL

Whew! I'm back. That was a really pretty walk around the block. Now, let's see where you are...

Guess what? You're doing it!

Go ahead, do a crazy dance – nobody's watching!

You've done a lot of work. I'm so incredibly proud of you.

You've identified and triaged the most important issues to deal with in your life, you've taken time to identify how you can take best care of yourself, you've worked on **forgiveness**, you've made connections to your **3-at-3**, you've cut out a lot of **negative people**, places and influences, you've developed your **gratitude** muscle, you've identified the optimum things to **change**, and what can stay the same, you've created a new way to talk about your former spouse, and even a **script** you're now saying to people who ask about them, you've written a list of new ideas to explore and **try** for your new **2.0 life**, you've learned the importance of a **laser focus**, and you've taken steps to accomplish **hard things**, and you're taking **baby steps** toward your big goals and **celebrating** yourself. Wow!

Like seriously, WOW! I'm so impressed!
That's A LOT for one person to accomplish and you're doing it! You're amazing!
You are honestly someone I want to meet.

"CELEBRATE GOOD TIMES, COME ON!"

In all sincerity, if you want to reach out to me, feel free to email me at Stacey@StaceyWaller.com. If you want to continue the journey and find out more about current How to Divorce Well courses, you can find that and plenty of additional free resources at www.StaceyWaller.com. See the QR code below

Also, you've graduated! Join me and other divorced men and women who are supporting one another on the Facebook page: How To Divorce Well. It's a place to be encouraged and to encourage others. You are not alone, and you can reach out to us on Facebook at all hours of the night.

And if this is the only thing you take away from this book, please remember:
You're just where you're supposed to be.
You're not alone.
You're healing and you may not even know it.
It won't always be like this.
You're going to be okay.

You're a hero!
Have you ever heard the saying, "Hurt people hurt people"? Well, it's also true that "Changed people change people!" That's YOU! You are growing and changing through this process.

I want to encourage you to consider becoming someone who builds others up by going through what you've experienced. Your experience and pain can help and inspire someone else, and there's always someone behind you in the process.

Want to know a little secret? Helping others on their journey will encourage YOU!

HOW TO DIVORCE WELL

After reading this book and using the tips and its worksheets, YOU are uniquely equipped to help someone else by just sharing your experience.

"Changed people change people!"
#HowToDivorceWell

God promises to return to you the years the locust have stolen.

Please stay in touch!

Big hugs,

P.S. If you have kids, I have a book called "How to Divorce Well for Parents." In it, we will journey together using many of the same tools we've learned in this book and find tangible tools to help our kids navigate this incredibly challenging season that they didn't ask for.
Love you!
XO,
S.

"CELEBRATE GOOD TIMES, COME ON!"

P.P.S. If this helped you, I'd love to know. My prayer I kept saying in the deepest times of pain and despair was, "God, please don't let my pain be in vain."

So when I wrote this book, it was with you in mind. I said, "Even if it helps one person, it will be worth it." If that's you, I'd love to hear from you.

Email me at:
stacey@staceywaller.com

EPILOGUE * "IS THAT YOU?"

On page 197 I asked the questions:

1. Do you feel like you know how it's going to work out? _____
2. Do you have a good idea what your life is going to look like in a year? _____
3. Do you believe, YOU may not know, but God does know how it's going to work out, and He has your best interest in mind? Answer honestly. No one but you will see this. Answer: _____ (maybe and kinda are sufficient answers).
4. Do you believe God can work everything together for good for those who know Him? _____
5. Is that you? _____

I pulled a quote out of a verse in the bible for that question. The actual verse reads like this: "All things work together for the good for those who know (God) and are called according to His purpose."

HOW TO DIVORCE WELL

But what about those who don't know God personally? Are you sure you are "called according to His purpose?" What does that even mean? It means living driven by the Spirit of God living inside of you. Do you have a relationship with God? Not a religion you belong to or a church you attend, but a relationship where you've handed the actual steering wheel of your life to God and you know His Spirit lives inside you?

If you don't, you can pray this right now:

Dear Lord Jesus, I know that I am a sinner, and I ask for Your forgiveness. I believe You died for my sins and rose from the dead. I turn from my sins and invite You to come into my heart and life. I want to trust and follow You as my Lord and Savior. Amen!

The way I said it was this…

"God, I can't do this on my own. I've tried. I'm not doing this perfectly. I am learning that having a relationship with you is not about me trying to do it all right and be approved by you.

But to have a relationship, You came to us. God, you had your Son born on earth. His name was Jesus. He was fully human and fully God and lead a perfect life. I understand that accepting his death as my payment for any of my deceptive and rebellious decisions ("sins"), I'm able to now have a relationship with you. Three days after He died, Jesus came back. He literally overcame death. That's how I can come to you. Because He is alive, He gave us His Spirit that embodies us, those who accept Your full payment as my way to God. Your Spirit inside me is what helps me turn away from my former life of sin, to lead a life that is the best version of myself.

EPILOGUE * "IS THAT YOU?"

Thank you for accepting me and coming into my life.

I hand over the steering wheel of my life to you.

I know me calling the shots with my best ideas and efforts isn't working. I want you in control of my life.

In Jesus' Name,
Amen

ABOUT THE AUTHOR

Stacey is a Southern California native who currently lives in Newport Beach, CA. She was married for 20 years and has two children. Stacey's parents divorced when she was 5 years old, and she mainly lived with her mom, with her dad being actively involved in her life. Growing up, she spent her summers and many holidays in the South with her father's side of the family, which is where her journey with faith began as a young child. She has deep ties to her Southern family.

She spent more than 20 years as a professional dancer and choreographer in Los Angeles, while also casting for television and film. She and her former husband owned ballroom dance studios in Los Angeles and traveled internationally, teaching swing, salsa, and ballroom. She successfully homeschooled two kids through high school, who have graduated from college and are enjoying successful careers.

During the divorce, she found herself alone, insecure, and jobless. While feeling vulnerable, betrayed, and afraid, it was hard to even look at people who were confident or succeeding. After all, they had a job and a clue of what they were doing the next day. On many days, she didn't.

As both a child of divorce and now having been through a divorce herself, she understands. She offers a unique perspective and the heart to give divorcees the tools, not only to survive, but to thrive on the other side of divorce.

Stacey Waller
www.StaceyWaller.com
email: Stacey@StaceyWaller.com

Facebook: How to Divorce Well - Shortening the Hurt Curve from Surviving to Thriving
Instagram: stacey_waller

Mailing Address
P.O. Box 52
Balboa Island, CA 92662
United States

ACKNOWLEDGEMENTS

From the bottom of my heart, thank you to...
My mom
My dad
Bill Holford
My Uncle Joe & Aunt Faye
Aunt Kathy Berg Bates
Aunt Betty Waller
Cousin Mark Waller
My 3-at-3
Nina Inman McCallie
Beth Silvey
Beverly Cooper
Christine Santana
Suzanne and Bill Wyrick
Alan and Tammy Caserio
Debbie Pickett
Carly Zamani
John and Sheila Noyes
Gay Tiss
Mike and Tanya Quon
Marianna Black Sparks
Brad and Julinda Den dulk
Jason and Melissa Sellers
Pastor Eric Heard
Dr. Cheri O'Nan
Robin Sateriale
Kimberly Garner

I love you

MEET WITH STACEY THROUGH

WEBINARS AND PODCASTS

- ✓ 1 year access to Webinars and Podcasts
- ✓ Invitation to Semi-Annual Zoom Coaching Session
- ✓ Access to private online Connection Circle Group

SMALL GROUP ZOOM COACHING

- ✓ All Webinars, Podcasts and Zoom Coaching Sessions (above)...PLUS
- ✓ 6 months of bi-weekly online meetings with a small group of women in similar stages
- ✓ 10 minute post-Zoom "Coaching Couch" Q&A time with Stacey
- ✓ 1 year access to all Masterclasses in parenting, finances, conflict resolution, and more...
- ✓ Access to private online Connection Circle Group

EXCLUSIVE VIP 1-ON-1**

- ✓ All Webinars, Podcasts and Zoom Coaching Sessions, access to "Coaching Couch," 1 year access to all Masterclasses and online Connection Circle (above)...PLUS
- ✓ 6 months of bi-weekly online meetings with small group coaching of women in similar stages...PLUS
- ✓ Personal sessions with Stacey, focused on your specific needs with a charted individualized plan
- ✓ 1 year access to all Masterclasses in parenting, finances, conflict resolution, and more...
- ✓ Ongoing access to Webinars, Podcasts and Group Zoom Coaching
- ✓ Access to private online Connection Circle Group

** Limited to 2 VIP clients per year

SIGN UP NOW!
www.StaceyWaller.com

as seen on

Stacey Waller
WALLER

Stacey Waller PO Box 52, Balboa Island, CA 92662

REFERENCES

NIV – New International Version
NASB – New American Standard Bible
MSG – The Message by Eugene Peterson
ESV – English Standard Version
NLT – New Living Translation

NASB
The New American Standard Bible. La Habra, CA: The Lockman Foundation, 2020.

NIV
The Holy Bible: New International Version. Grand Rapids: Zondervan, 2011.

ESV
The Holy Bible: English Standard Version. Wheaton, IL: Crossway, 2016.

NLT
The Holy Bible: New Living Translation. Carol Stream, IL: Tyndale House Publishers, 2015.

MSG
Peterson, Eugene. "The Message: The Bible in Contemporary Language". Colorado Springs: NavPress, 2020.

Stanley, Charles. "In His Presence". Nashville: Thomas Nelson, 2023.

Healthline Magazine. "Worried Sick: Health, Anxiety, The 'Do-I-Have-This? Disorder". Em Burfitt. September 3, 2019.

Gaiman, Neil. The Sandman: Preludes & Nocturnes. New York: DC Comics, 1991.

Leaf, Caroline. "How to Build Mental Toughness." Dr. Leaf, November 14, 2018.

Merriam-Webster, Inc. *Merriam-Webster's Collegiate Dictionary*. 11th ed. Springfield, MA: Merriam-Webster, 2003.

Dallas Whole Life Counseling. "Study on Divorce Statistics"https://dallaswholelife.com/tag/statistics/ Plano, TX: Dallas Whole Life Counseling, 2019.

p. 43 quote from Pastor Mike Todd's series *Forgiveness University*.

p.59 Dr. Karen Swartz, director of the Mood Disorders Adult Consultation Clinic at Johns Hopkins writes many articles on health benefits of forgiveness including https://www.artoflivingwell.org/blog/power-offorgiveness

REFERENCES

Hyatt, Michael, and Daniel Harkavy. *Living Forward: A Proven Plan to Stop Drifting and Get the Life You Want.* Grand Rapids: Baker Books, 2016.

Scott, Robia. *Counterfeit Comforts: Freedom from the Imposters That Keep You from True Peace, Purpose and Passion.* Grand Rapids: Chosen Books, 2016.

NOTES

 Ultimate World Publishing
Diamond Creek,
Victoria Australia 3089
www.writeabook.com.au

www.ingramcontent.com/pod-product-compliance
Lightning Source LLC
Chambersburg PA
CBHW030256100526
44590CB00012B/423